Join the Club

Idioms for Academic and Social Success

Lisa Naylor

McGraw-Hill
Contemporary

McGraw-Hill/Contemporary

A Division of The McGraw-Hill Companies

Join the Club 1, 1st Edition

Printed in the United States of America.

1 2 3 4 5 6 7 8 9 10   XXX   07 06 05 04 03 02 01

ISBN: 0-07-242795-7
ISBN: 0-07-112386-5 (ISE)

Editorial Director: *Tina B. Carver*
Developmental Editor: *Louis Carrillo*
Director of Marketing: *Thomas P. Dare*
Production Manager: *Genevieve Kelley*
Interior Designer: *Michael Warrell, Design Solutions*
Compositor: *Tracey Harris*
Typeface: *10/13 Palatino*
Printer:

TABLE OF CONTENTS

CHAPTER 4

in the same boat, look forward to, backseat driver, get over, down-to-earth, see someone, get together, in hot water, sweet tooth, hang on, blind date, go through, open-minded, make good time, give it a shot

CHAPTER 5

hunk, talk someone's ears off, come in handy, get along, long time no see, ring a bell, come over, a morning/night person, figure out, have it together, pushy, lemon, break up, get in shape, on someone's back

CHAPTER 6

know-it-all, stress out, neat, have a crush on someone, easy come easy go, shape up or ship out, be into, steal, run into, fake, folks, show up, stuck-up, stick with it, play the field

CHAPTER 7

knockout, come up with, hot, hit the sack, keep an eye on, chicken, take turns, nosy, drop off, back in a flash, work out, step on it, loaded, brain, put your foot in your mouth

CHAPTER **8**   turn down, call it a day/night, lend a hand, wild, shortcut,
have time to kill, bummer, luck out, get even, fish for compliments,
sixth sense, get it, climb the walls, straighten up, tough

CHAPTER **9**   count on, weird, the works, better late than never, have had it,
sweetheart, turn in, fed up with, out in left field, wishy-washy,
for real, have something wired, fill in, creepy, a blast

TO THE TEACHER

Level 1

Join the Club: Idioms for Academic and Social Success was written for low-intermediate to advanced nonnative speakers of English. Level 1 is intended for low-intermediate to intermediate levels. Level 2 is intended for high-intermediate to advanced levels. Each level was written with a two-part objective. The first part is to introduce students to the most frequently occurring idiomatic expressions; in other words, the colloquial speech actually heard outside the classroom. Because of the frequency of expressions, included in some chapters are slang expressions which have been selected for their saliency and "safeness," such as **neat** or **cool**.

The second part of the objective is to foster communicative competence through engaging students in integrated skills tasks. Not only do students practice the expressions through listening, speaking, reading and writing activities, but they are also given opportunities to discuss and reflect on the sociolinguistic features generally associated with the expressions. This helps to raise register awareness of the language: who uses the expressions (young, old, male, female, etc), in which types of situations the expressions are used (at school, at work, among friends, etc.), and how the expressions are used (happy, upset, neutral, etc). For example, **keep your fingers crossed** is an expression that almost everyone of all ages uses. **Stress out** is an expression that is widely used at work or school. **Crack up** is an expression that is naturally said in a happy tone of voice. Students greatly appreciate being exposed to such meaningful and useful information about their second language and the society in which it is spoken. This not only helps them to communicate more naturally with native speakers through using such high-frequency expressions but also to develop an awareness of sociocultural expectations as well as to discriminate among individuals they may encounter in their second-language environment.

Join the Club was designed to access all learner styles and to be student-centered. The activities in the book revolve around students working together to maximize cooperative learning. However, many of the activities are also suitable for the student who prefers to work alone. Suggestions for grouping students are provided although effective student grouping is ultimately left to the discretion of the instructor. Many students naturally self-group as they progress through the chapters. Because the book is student-centered, the teacher is free to circulate around the classroom and give more individualized attention.

There are 135 expressions presented explicitly in nine chapters, which consist of 15 expressions each. In addition to the target expressions in each chapter, there are related expressions explained in Part III of each chapter as well as more expressions used in context. Every expression can be found in the Index/Glossary, which has a total of 242 expressions.

After every three chapters there is a review. Each chapter follows a consistent five-part design to systematically introduce, practice, and apply the 15 expressions. The 15 expressions are divided into groups of 5, which represent a variety of grammatical categories (verbs, phrasal verbs, nouns, adjectives, adverbs). Following are suggestions for use:

■ Part I

Work It Out—Grouping Strategy: Divide the students into groups 1, 2 and 3. For example, Student Group 1 studies the five expressions on pages 2–3. Student Group 2 studies the five expressions on pages 4–5. Student Group 3 studies the expressions on pages 6–7. Explain to the students that, in their group, they will study five new expressions and complete four exercises together. The four exercises are

1) **Quick Fix**—match the expressions to the words that are similar.

2) **Cloze It**—read the sentence and fill in the blank with the appropriate expression while paying attention to grammar requirements.

3) **Sense or Nonsense**—discuss the sentences and decide if they do or don't make sense (i.e., I'm broke again! It's time to go to Las Vegas and hit the casinos!).

4) **Plug In**—replace the underlined phrases with the appropriate expressions while observing grammar requirements. (15-20 minutes)

■ Part II

Information Gap—This is the trickiest part of the book, but please note that after one chapter, most students understand the logic behind the design of the book.

Grouping Strategy: After each student group has studied 5 expressions, re-group the students so that all three groups are working together. Because the purpose of the **Information Gap** is to maximize meaning negotiation through listening to and verifying what each other said, the instructor must explain to the students that

• they will be introduced to the other 10 expressions of the chapter by testing a classmate who has just studied them, and

• it is very important that they look at their assigned pages to fully benefit from this activity. For example, Student 1 will look at pages 2–3 while Student 2 and Student 3 ask the **Information Gap** questions on page 8. Student 1 must listen and explain to Students 2 and 3, who write down the answers as given.

The two Information Gap tasks are (1) **Tell Me**—students directly ask for the expression and write it down, and (2) **Make This Make Sense**—students have to figure out a way to make the sentence make sense, usually through changing one or two words. As the instructor circulates around the classroom, it's a great idea to encourage the students to look for more than one way to make the sentences make sense. This not only invites discussion among the students, but also reinforces grammar and vocabulary knowledge.

After the three rounds of the **Information Gap** are completed, tell the students they must complete all of Part I of the chapter. This may be assigned as an in-class assignment or for homework. Tell them to consult Appendix B—the Answer Key. (15—20 minutes)

It's Halftime—There are four Halftime Activities, which begin with the **Expression Guide**, the purpose of which is to initiate a discussion about register. Students will follow three questions to talk about how, when, where and by whom the expressions may be used. This can be assigned as homework to be done with native speakers outside the classroom, or it can be done in-class as a whole- or a small-group activity. The instructor may wish to make an overhead of the **Expression Guide** on which to write any important sociolinguistic features which pertain to certain expressions. For example, the expression **What a bummer** may be said in a frustrated tone of voice. Encourage the students to fill the **Expression Guide** up with any meaningful information about the expressions and share what they discover with each other.

The **Expression Guide** is also an ideal activity for the instructor to invite the students to compare expressions in their own culture to those they are studying. The instructor may also wish to expand on some meanings of the expressions as they come up. For example, the slang item **jock** has a derogatory meaning, but not all the time. Some sports fans may wish they were jocks, and there is nothing necessarily derogatory about that! Encourage the students to think and ask questions. For example, a student may ask if a person can be **a lemon**. The instructor can explain that normally a lemon is a faulty car or appliance although it can certainly be humorous to call a person a lemon. Make sure the students understand why that could be funny. (10—30 minutes, depending on the class).

The next activity, **Circle and Discuss**, is a reading/vocabulary activity in which the students may work in pairs or in small groups to read the sentences together in order to circle the key words and phrases that illustrate the meaning of the target expression. This task is designed to present the expressions in a context to increase and recycle vocabulary and to embed further meaning. Be sure to encourage the students to discuss what they are reading by prompting them with questions. Consider the following example from Chapter 7:

Soccer is definitely the **hottest** sport in the world even though baseball and football are much more popular in the United States.

As the instructor circulates around the room, he or she may ask, "What do you think about soccer, football, and baseball? Are they popular in your country?" While circulating from group to group, the instructor can simply point to any of the sentences the group has been working on and ask what they think. (10—15 minutes)

The third activity, **Find Out**, is a focussed grammar and/or meaning expansion. Any expression which carries important grammatical information and/or further meaning is presented, explained, and followed up by related question to be completed by the student. There is also a Grammar Guide in Appendix E for more in-depth grammar explanations.
(10 minutes)

The final Halftime Activity is the **Expression Log**. This is a two-part activity which should be completed out of class. The students should keep their **Expression Log** in a small notebook, which the instructor will collect to provide feedback and return to the students. In the first part, the students are asked to choose any 10 expressions from the chapter to write original sentences which demonstrate that they understand the meaning of the expression. The instructor may suggest that the students personalize their sentences to increase memory retention. It is also a great idea to encourage the students to use more than one expression in a sentence or even to write several paragraphs to create a meaningful context. This provides students with the opportunity to be creative and write stories! Students can also share what they write with their classmates, which is a very enjoyable expansion to the first part of the **Expression Log**.

The second part of the **Expression Log** is to have the students record a minimum of two new expressions following the **New Expression Guide** in Appendix A. They can keep track of their expressions on the **New Expression List** also located in Appendix A. Because the **Expression Log** is a natural place to provide students with further individualized attention, the instructor should encourage the students to communicate any questions about the expressions they may have.

It is very important for the instructor to collect, correct, and return the **Expression Logs** to the students. It is also recommended to keep an on-going list of the new expressions the students bring to class. At some point during the term, the instructor may compile on a class list the new expressions brought in by the students. The students can then review their **Logs** in order to teach their particular expressions on the class list to their classmates. The expressions may also be used for an optional final activity (further described in Appendix D—the Suggestion Box), which is to have the students write a chapter following the chapter format.

■ Part IV

Tune In—Now that the students have studied the expressions, it is time to apply them. The **Tune In** listening tasks, of which there are nine variations, are designed to make the students apply the expressions through either contextualized meaning expansion (i.e., listening for contextual clues which elicit the expression) or listening for meaning (i.e., did that make sense, was the expression used properly?). The transcripts for the **Tune In** tasks are in Appendix C.

Before doing a **Tune In** listening task, be sure to read over the instructions with the students to make sure they understand. Allow time for them to look over the format, and explain that they will be able to listen to the activity two or three times (left to the discretion of the instructor). It is also recommended to do the first two questions together as a whole class to make sure that the students understand the objective of the activity. After each **Tune In**, be sure to allow time for student discussion. (15—20 minutes)

■ Part V

The Chat Room—There are also nine variations to this final chapter activity, which is a conversational board game designed to maximize turn taking with the roll of the die and an optional minute timer. The instructor may want to use the minute timer for the group that has a combination of gregarious and reticent students. By circulating and listening to the students during **The Chat Room** activity, the instructor can also ascertain how well the students have learned the target expressions of each chapter. If supplemental practice is needed, the instructor may consult Appendix D—the Suggestion Box—for ideas. (20—25 minutes)

Reviews: After every three chapters, there is a four-part Review designed to practice all the expressions of the preceding chapters. The first activity is a game, such as Tic-Tac-Toe or Password. The second activity is a **Dialogue Match** in which students work in pairs to find the sequence of the dialogue. The instructor may require the students to role-play the **Dialogue Match** or even memorize and recite it. The third activity revolves around meaning negotiation, and the fourth activity requires that the students, in groups of two or three, use a minimum of 20 expressions in either a story or dialogue. The instructor may want to build the final review activity into a class contest, set categories for winning, and even arrange it so that everyone wins. For example:

1) Which group used the most expressions?

2) Which group had the best grammar?

3) Which group was the funniest?

4) Which group was the most interesting?

The instructor can also have the students design a classbook based on the Grand Finale, the final review activity. Classbook ideas can be found in Appendix D—the Suggestion Box.

General Notes

Pronunciation: Every activity in **Join the Club** has been designed to maximize cooperative learning by integrating the skills of listening, speaking, reading, and writing through building upon meaning negotiation, vocabulary expansion, and grammar reinforcement. There are several ways to integrate pronunciation in every chapter. First of all, after the students have finished **Parts I** and **II**, the instructor can say each expression and read some of the exercises using the expressions. The students can repeat after the instructor, which also lets them review what they have just studied. The sentences in **Part III Circle and Discuss** may also be used the same way. This traditional listen and repeat pronunciation exercise provides an opportunity to practice the important elements of contractions, reductions, and deletions in English pronunciation. It also provides useful intonation practice. This not only gives students a chance to be expressive but also helps them to recognize thought groups and focus words. If instructors choose to practice pronunciation in this manner, remember to be as animated as possible so that the students can hear these elements of pronunciation. Also, because **Join the Club** is a student-centered textbook, the instructor may choose to address pronunciation on an individualized basis while circulating around the classroom. One last suggestion for practicing pronunciation is to have the students perform the Dialogue Matches and Grand Finale stories from the Chapter Reviews. These are great for reviewing expressions as well as for practicing pronunciation.

Selection of Expressions: Every expression in **Join the Club** has been carefully researched and selected for its saliency and high-frequency use. This was done over years of teaching idioms and slang both in the United States and overseas. all of the expressions come from students who read or heard them somewhere—in a class, at work, from a friend, while traveling, from a movie, a TV show, a song, the radio, the newspaper, a magazine, a novel, etc. I compiled a master list of all the expressions the students came up with, no matter how many times they occurred. For example, in one year alone, over 126 students heard **check it out.**

After choosing the most frequently occurring expressions, I consulted several specialized dictionaries for the purpose of building in the sociolinguistic aspect to **Join the Club**. I wanted to verify if the expressions were idioms, slang words, jargon, argot, colloquialisms, vernacularisms, proverbs, formal or informal language, etc. Because it is the nature of language to overlap in defining if a particular expression is, for example, an idiom or a colloquialism, for the purpose of **Join the Club**, I decided to simplify and label only the slang items.

Finally, the expressions in each chapter were purposely not chosen to fit into a particular theme. If a textbook is organized using a theme-based approach, expressions are selected for the sake of the theme rather than their saliency or frequency of use. If native speakers rarely use such expressions, why make students learn them? As previously mentioned, every expression in **Join the Club** was selected for its saliency and high frequency and the expressions for each chapter were chosen based on their grammatical category as well as their semantic features. In every chapter there is a variety of verbs, phrasal verbs, nouns, adjectives, adverbs and phrases which carry a variety of meaning associations: positive, negative, funny, serious, neutral, etc. The rationale behind this type of selection of expressions is based on first-language acquisition theory: provide the learner with a rich variety of lexical items from which to choose to create and embed meaning. I'm confident that when your students write their **Expression Logs**, that when you listen to them engage in meaning negotiation activities, such as **Sense or Nonsense**, **Make this Make Sense**, **Circle and Discuss**, and **The Chat Room**, you will be very pleased with the results!

A Special Note For English-as-a-Foreign-Language Instructors: Whether you are a native speaker or a non-native speaker, one of the biggest challenges in teaching EFL is not only finding authentic material to use in the classroom, but also finding native speakers or fluent speakers with whom your students can practice. In Part III of every chapter, I suggest making the **Expression Guide** a whole class or small group activity. For students to complete the second part of the **Expression Log**, both you and your students can bring into the classroom whatever is available in English on the radio, in music, on television, at the movies, in an English language newspaper, magazine or book, and on the Internet, and so on.

–LN

TO THE STUDENT

Welcome to **Join the Club!** Every language has many idioms and slang expressions. I wrote this book to introduce you to the English that you hear or see every day outside the classroom—from friends, acquaintances, at the movies, in a song, on the radio, in the newspaper, in a magazine, or on the Internet! Because the expressions in this book are so common, you may have heard many of them already. But do you know what they mean? Do you know how to use them?

There are three goals of **Join the Club.** You will:

1) learn the expressions by understanding the meaning and grammar,

2) practice using the expressions in different situations, and

3) look for more expressions outside the classroom on your own by keeping an **Expression Log**, which is a notebook of your own personal practice.

Every chapter in **Join the Club** has five parts. It is better to work with your classmates to complete most of the parts, but you can also work alone. To learn and practice the expressions so that you can remember them, you will do listening, speaking, reading, and writing exercises and play games. You will also practice grammar and use a lot of vocabulary to learn the expressions. It's important to complete all the activities in every chapter so that you'll be able to remember the expressions to use them when you want to.

You should always check your answers in the Answer Key in Appendix B. If you have grammar questions, you can look at the Grammar Guide in Appendix E. If you have questions about the meaning of some expressions, you can look in the Index/Glossary in Appendix F.

Be sure to ask your teacher, friends, or acquaintances any questions you may have.

–LN

ACKNOWLEDGEMENTS

I would like to thank the Intensive English Language Program at the University of California, San Diego for giving me the opportunity to write **Join the Club**. I would like to express my gratitude to the Director, Mr. Peter Thomas, and the Assistant Director, Ms. Roxanne Nuhaily, who believed in the concept of this textbook and awarded me a leave of absence from work in order to write it.

A special thank you goes to my colleagues who used the book in its various drafts in their classrooms and provided me with valuable feedback. In particular, I'd like to thank Annette Gonhes, Michael Rose, Brian McDonald, and Gonzalo Peralta.

I would also like to thank the people at McGraw-Hill for being so enthusiastic about **Join the Club**.

Finally, a huge thank you to all my students everywhere! You are the ones who discovered all the expressions in **Join the Club** because you turned in your Expression Logs. You opened your ears and your eyes to make the English around you come alive. This book is for you.

–LN

1

grab a bite

awesome

a buddy

bucks

be broke

be nuts about

check out

no big deal

crack up

keep your fingers crossed

a jerk

kidding

feel like

hang out

cool

Student Group 1

Learn the meanings of the following five expressions by completing the exercises. Work with Student Group 1 or by yourself.

■ **GUESS** the meanings of the five expressions.

1) It's **no big deal**! Don't worry about it.

2) Let's **grab a bite**! I'm hungry and I'm in a hurry.

3) I'm **nuts about** her! She's always on my mind. I can't stop thinking about her

4) Let's **check out** that new Thai restaurant.

5) Bill Gates makes big **bucks**. He can buy whatever he wants.

■ **CHECK OUT** the definitions and examples of the expressions.

1) **no big deal**—not important, no need to worry, no problem.
   Lisa: "Sorry I'm late. I got stuck in traffic."
   *Russell: "It's **no big deal**. I just got here too!"*

2) **grab a bite**—eat something quickly in a short period of time.
   Kim: "We have to get to the post office before it closes, but I'm starving."
   *Cory: "So am I. Let's **grab a bite** at MacDonald's—it's on the way."*

3) **nuts about**—really like someone or something a lot.
   *Yoko is **nuts about** living in California. I think she's going to stay here as long as she can.*

4) **check out**—go and see what someone or something is about, get information.
   *Dennis wants to **check out** the Sony DVD player at the electronics store.*

5) **bucks**—money.
   *Carlo bought a great used car for only $1,500 **bucks**!*

■ **QUICK FIX**—Match the expressions to the words that are similar.

1) like a lot   ___bucks

2) eat quickly   ___be nuts about

3) dollars   ___check out

4) no worries   ___grab a bite

5) see what's happening   ___no big deal

■ **CLOZE IT**—Use one of the above expressions to complete the sentences. Be sure to check your grammar!

1) Let's _____the movie theater that just opened.

2) We missed the first part of the meeting, but it was_____.

3) I'd better_____before my next class so I won't get hungry.

4) Elizabeth is completely _____Michael. She can't stop smiling!

5) Give me a couple of _____and I'll buy some lotto tickets.

■ **SENSE OR NONSENSE**—With your classmates, discuss the sentences and decide if they do or don't make sense.

1) Marc makes such big **bucks** that he paid cash for a brand new Porsche._____

2) It's **no big deal** if you miss all of your tests._____

3) Juan is **nuts about** Gloria. He never wants to see her again._____

4) We **grabbed a bite** at Chez La France for about four hours._____

5) Do you want to go **check out** some new music at Tower Records with me?_____

■ **PLUG IT IN**—Use the expressions to replace the underlined words. Make sure to check your grammar! Check the Index/Glossary for words you may not know.

1) Samuel is <u>falling in love with</u> Michelle.

2) <u>Don't worry about it</u> if you mail it after Friday. It will get there before Wednesday.

3) Let's <u>eat</u> at Easy Burger before we get on the freeway and hit the rush hour traffic!

4) Bruce told me that he would love to <u>see</u> more of Europe next summer.

5) I wouldn't leave you for a million <u>dollars</u> because I'm totally nuts about you!

Student Group 2

Learn the meanings of the following five expressions by completing the exercises. Work with Student Group 2 or by yourself.

■ **GUESS** the meanings of the five expressions.

1) Ha Ha—I'm just **kidding**!

2) That comedian really **cracks me up**.

3) The Grand Canyon is an **awesome** place.

4) That **jerk** was totally rude to us!

5) I hope you win! I'll **keep my fingers crossed**.

■ **CHECK OUT** the definitions and examples of the expressions.

1) **kidding**—joke with or tease someone for fun, say something that may not be true.
   *Are you **kidding** me? I can't believe it!*

2) **crack up**—laugh, make someone laugh.
   *When Bob told that joke, everyone **cracked up**!*

3) **awesome**—very impressive, magnificent, wonderful, great.
   *Mariah Carey has an **awesome** voice.*

4) **a jerk**—a person who is rude, insensitive, or annoying.
   *Steve left Sue sitting all alone in the restaurant. What a **jerk**!*

5) **keep one's fingers crossed**—hope for good luck, wish someone good luck.
   *Keep your fingers crossed for me! I'm taking *the bar!*
   **a very difficult test that people must take to become a lawyer*

■ **QUICK FIX**—Match the expressions to the words that are similar.

1) amazing   ___kidding

2) insensitive person   ___cross one's fingers

3) laugh   ___awesome

4) not really true   ___jerk

5) wish for good luck   ___crack up

■ **CLOZE IT**—Use one of the above expressions to complete the sentences. Be sure to check your grammar!

1) I can't believe he abandoned his wife and kids. What a_____!

2) Guess what?! I won the lottery! Not really. I'm _____.

3) Jimi Hendricks was an _____guitarist.

4) Emily _____us_____with all the funny voices she can make.

5) Let's _____and play some craps in Las Vegas.

■ **SENSE OR NONSENSE**—With your classmates, discuss the sentences and decide if they do or don't make sense.

1) Dean is a very serious and quiet guy. He is always **kidding** about something._____

2) **Jerks** are great people to have as friends._____

3) I feel like seeing a comedy tonight because I want to **crack up**._____

4) Paul **kept his fingers crossed** and was glad that we lost._____

5) Rome is one of the most **awesome** cities in the world.___

■ **PLUG IT IN**—Use the expressions to replace the underlined words. Make sure to check your grammar! Check the Index/Glossary for words you may not know.

1) The comedy club was hysterical. We couldn't stop <u>laughing</u>!

2) I <u>really wish you all the best</u> for your promotion at work.

3) Harold was such <u>a fool</u> for being so self-centered.

4) Southern Utah has some of the most <u>breathtaking</u> scenery in the world.

5) No way! You must be *<u>pulling my leg</u>*. You're trying to trick me.

Student Group 3

Learn the meanings of the following five expressions by completing the exercises. Work with Student Group 3 or by yourself.

■ **GUESS** the meanings of the five expressions.

1) I **feel like** seeing a movie tonight.

2) Todd **is broke**. He spent his whole paycheck again.

3) Luke and Lani love to **hang out** at the beach and watch all the people.

4) Fred and Bruno have been good **buddies** since high school.

5) That is so **cool** that you won a free trip to New York.

■ **CHECK OUT** the definitions and examples of the expressions.

1) **feel like**—want to do, would like.
   Do you feel like having sushi tonight?

2) **be broke**—not have any or enough money.
   We spent all our cash on a new car. Now we're broke.

3) **hang out**—spend time somewhere, socialize.
   Yoshi wants to hang out with Americans so he can speak more English.

4) **a buddy**—a friend.
   Dave is my surfing buddy.

5) **cool**—fine, great, terrific.
   PageMaker is a cool software program for Web Publishing.

■ **QUICK FIX**—Match the expressions to the words that are similar.

1) spend time   ___cool

2) no money   ___hang out

3) super   ___feel like

4) a pal   ___be broke

5) would like   ___a buddy

■ **CLOZE IT**—Use one of the above expressions to complete the sentences. Be sure to check your grammar!

1) _____ with me and we'll have a lot of fun together.

2) Ken and Tolga have become good golf_____.

3) Penny told me that she_____ going clothes shopping.

4) Your new surround sound stereo is really _____. It sounds great!

5) I can't take a vacation this year because I_____.

■ **SENSE OR NONSENSE**—With your classmates, discuss the sentences and decide if they do or don't make sense.

1) Julie and I met each other in high school and have been good **buddies** ever since._____

2) Traveling in a new country and learning the language can be a very **cool** experience._____

3) I'm **broke** again. It's time to go to Las Vegas and hit the casinos._____

4) I usually **feel like** having dessert after dinner._____

5) Curt can't stand **hanging out with** his girlfriend._____

■ **PLUG IT IN**—Use the expressions to replace the underlined words. Make sure to check your grammar!   Check the Index/Glossary for words you may not know.

1) Doug <u>is interested in</u> learning more about the stockmarket.

2) We decided to <u>stay</u> in Seattle for a few more days because it was so beautiful.

3) It's super interesting to become <u>friends</u> with all the different people in my class.

4) We <u>don't have much money</u> right now because we just bought new furniture.

5) That would be <u>fantastic</u> if you visit us this summer.

PART II Information Gap

Questions to Ask Someone from Student Group 1

Ask Student 1 the following questions. He or she will tell you the answers. You should write down the answers. Student 1 can look at pages 2-3 to find the answers.

■ **TELL ME:** Ask Student 1 the following questions to get the expressions.

1) How can I tell someone not to worry about something?_____

2) What is an informal word for money?_____

3) What is a way to say that you really, really like someone?_____

4) I want to eat something quickly before class. How can I say this?_____

5) What can I say if I want to go to a place I've never been before?_____

■ **MAKE THIS MAKE SENSE:** Ask Student 1 to change these sentences to make sense.

1) I don't want to **hang out** with him because I'm nuts about him.

2) If you travel, you won't **check out** new places.

3) It's **no big deal** that you burned my house down!

4) If you want to make some big **bucks**, don't work.

5) We usually **grab a bite** for holiday meals with family and friends.

Questions to Ask Someone from Student Group 2

Ask Student 2 the following questions. He or she will tell you the answers. You should write down the answers. Student 2 can look at pages 4-5 to find the answers.

■ **TELL ME:** Ask Student 2 the following questions to get the expressions.

1) How should I tell someone that I was only joking?_____

2) How can I describe something amazing?_____

3) What can I say to wish someone good luck?_____

4) What can I say if a joke makes me laugh hard?_____

5) Is there a strong way to describe someone who acts like a fool?_____

■ **MAKE THIS MAKE SENSE:** Ask Student 2 to change these sentences to make sense.

1) I'll **keep my fingers crossed** that you won't get that job you want.

2) Tom is so serious that he's always **kidding** about everything.

3) That comedy really **cracks me up** because it is so boring.

4) Pat is nuts about John because he is such **a jerk**.

5) Cleaning the house is a really **awesome** way to spend the weekend.

Questions to Ask Someone from Student Group 3

Ask Student 3 the following questions. He or she will tell you the answers. You should write down the answers. Student 3 can look at pages 6-7 to find the answers.

■ **TELL ME:** Ask Student 3 following questions to get the expressions.

1) How can I say that I like to spend time with my friends?_____

2) What is a popular way to say something is great?_____

3) What is another way to call someone who is a good friend?_____

4) Is there a way to say that I want to do something?_____

5) How can I explain that I don't have enough money?_____

■ **MAKE THIS MAKE SENSE:** Ask Student 3 to change these sentences to make sense.

1) I never **feel like** going to sleep when I'm tired.

2) Daniel and I are great **buddies**. We just met last week.

3) Scott **is broke**, so he pays for everything with cash.

4) It's not fun to **hang out** at the beach when the weather is great.

5) John Travolta doesn't seem like a very **cool** guy.

Students 1—2—3

Before you begin the Halftime Activities, you must first complete pages 2-10 of Chapter 1. These activities are designed to get you to think about and discuss the meaning and use of the 15 expressions you have just studied.

■ **EXPRESSION GUIDE:** With your class, in small groups, or with friends, look over and talk about the idioms and slang you've been studying. Write down any extra information. Here are some questions to ask each other:

1) What kinds of people do you think use these expressions?
   (young, old, male, female...)

2) Where do you think you might hear these expressions?
   (school, beach, home, work, restaurant, nightclub, store...)

3) How do you think people say these expressions?
   (happy, angry, neutral, excited...)

EXPRESSION GUIDE

no big deal	grab a bite	be nuts about	check out	bucks
kidding	crack up	awesome *slang*	a jerk *slang*	keep your fingers crossed
feel like	be broke	hang out	a buddy	cool *slang*

■ CIRCLE AND DISCUSS key words or phrases that show the meaning of the expression. Be sure to work with a partner.

1) I didn't have enough time for breakfast or lunch today! Now I only have 15 minutes before my next class so I'm going to **grab a bite** at the cafeteria.

2) What? Are you **kidding** me? I can't believe it! That's nuts!

3) I **feel like** going dancing tonight. I haven't been out for a long time.

4) Jason and Sabine **are nuts about** each other. They're always together holding hands, giggling, and making goo-goo eyes at each other!

5) Marco and Nick have been basketball **buddies** since they were kids. They still play every week.

6) If we get all the answers right, we'll win a trip to Hawaii! So **keep your fingers crossed** for us.

7) We're going to **check out** that new shopping center this weekend to see what's there. Do you want to come with us?

8) Seeing the waterfalls in Yosemite National Park after it rains is **awesome**.

9) Arzu and Tomoyo usually **hang out** at the gym cafe and drink fresh fruit smoothies after they work out.

10) Don't worry about forgetting my birthday. It's really **no big deal**. I'll probably forget yours too!

11) Tim told me that when he invited Tina over to his house for dinner, she wouldn't stay because she didn't like his house. Can you believe what **a jerk** she was to him?

12) Alberto certainly seems to make big **bucks** because he's always loaded with cash and he always treats everyone to lunch.

13) Sorry. I can't go hot air ballooning this weekend. It's too expensive for me right now because I just paid my school tuition and I**'m broke**.

14) Michael is definitely one of the funniest people I know. He can **crack anyone up** with all those faces he makes.

15) Our new offices are going to be really **cool**. Everyone will have new furniture, a new computer, and a better phone system!

■ **FIND OUT** about some grammar points and additional meanings of some expressions. Consult the Grammar Guide in Appendix E on page 181 for more information.

1) check out—The phrasal verb **check out** has two meanings. In this chapter, you learned that **check out** means to discover, examine, get information about or look over something or someone. In this meaning, **check out** is a separable phrasal verb:

   a) Let's go **check out** <u>the waves</u>!

   b) Let's go **check** <u>the waves</u> out!

   *c) Let's go **check** <u>them</u> out!

   *Grammar rule: If the object of a phrasal verb is a pronoun, you must separate the verb and the particle.

   The second common meaning of **check out** is to pay the bill and leave a hotel. In this case, **check out** is an inseparable phrasal verb.

   d) We have to check out by 11:00 a.m.

   Rewrite the following sentence by putting the object of **check out** into the corresponding pronoun form: We checked out <u>the new computer superstore</u> last weekend. (object)

   e) _____.

2) crack up—The phrasal verb **crack up** can be separable or inseparable. When it means to laugh, it is inseparable (intransitive—has no object). When it means to make someone laugh, it is separable (transitive—has an object). For example:

   a) Kim **cracks up** every time she sees Kevin because he **cracks her up**.

   (inseparable)   (separable)

   You can also make **crack up** into a noun by using an article, as in **a crack up**. Answer the following question by using **crack up** as a noun.

   Why does Kim laugh whenever she sees Kevin?

   b) _____.

3) feel like—The verb phrase **feel like** requires either a noun or gerund phrase to follow. For example:

   a) **I feel like** <u>pizza</u> for dinner tonight.

   (noun phrase)

   b) **I feel like** <u>buying some new clothes</u>.

   (gerund phrase)

   Now it's your turn:

   a) **I feel like** _____.

   (noun phrase)

   b) **I feel like** _____.

   (gerund phrase)

4) nuts about—While **nuts about** means to really like someone or something, the word **nut** has a few different meanings in English. Below are two common expressions:

   a) She is **nuts** to marry him. She's only known him for three days! She's crazy!

   b) My neighbor must be some kind of **a nut**—he painted his whole house black! He's bizarre, weird, strange...

   Write an original sentence using one of the new meanings of **nut**:

   *c)*_____.

5) kidding—Two other very common expressions using the word **kidding** are **no kidding** and **I'm not kidding**. They both mean really or honestly, but **I'm not kidding** is more serious. For example:

   a) They're getting a divorce? **No kidding**!

   b) Turn that music down! **I'm not kidding**!

   Use **no kidding** or **I'm not kidding** to respond to the following:

   c) Please don't call me so early in the morning. _____!

   d) They're moving to Hawaii?_____!

6) jerk—The slang word **jerk** is negative and can be rude. If you want to use this word, be careful who you say it to!

   a) Can I call my boss a jerk?_____

   b) Should I call a police officer a jerk?_____

   c) Can I call my teacher a jerk?_____

7) buddy—A person, usually a man, who you don't know can be called **buddy** or **bud**, but **it's often** in an unfriendly way. For example:

   a) Hey **buddy**—watch where you're driving!

   Decide if the following are friendly or unfriendly.

   b) Dorothy is a **buddy** of mine._____

   c) Look out **bud**! You almost *ran into* me!_____

■ **EXPRESSION LOG:** (1) Choose 10 expressions from this chapter to practice by writing original sentences, then (2) add two new expressions that you hear. Follow the New Expression Guide in Appendix A on page 159.

■ **LISTEN** to your teacher tell stories using the key words in the boxes below. In each box, write the expression that is being described.

1. fabulous	**2. best wishes**	**3. in the mood for**
Expression _____	*Expression* _____	*Expression* _____
_____	_____	_____
_____	_____	_____
4. evaluate	**5. pal**	**6. laugh till you cry**
Expression _____	*Expression* _____	*Expression* _____
_____	_____	_____
_____	_____	_____
7. socialize	**8. crazy about**	**9. idiot**
Expression _____	*Expression* _____	*Expression* _____
_____	_____	_____
_____	_____	_____
10. cash	**11. eat fast**	**12. joking**
Expression _____	*Expression* _____	*Expression* _____
_____	_____	_____
_____	_____	_____
13. don't worry	**14. can't buy**	**15. neat**
Expression _____	*Expression* _____	*Expression* _____
_____	_____	_____
_____	_____	_____

Start by rolling the die and by writing your name(s) in the corresponding box depending on the number you rolled. Then go to the question below with the same number and answer it using the expression indicated. Continue around the board until you've answered all the questions. Use the boxes where you write your name as a place marker.

1.	2.	3.	4.	5.
Names	Names	Names	Names	Names
6.	7.	8.	9.	10.
Names	Names	Names	Names	Names
11.	12.	13.	14.	15.
Names	Names	Names	Names	Names

1. Where do you usually **grab a bite** when you're in a hurry?

2. When was the last time you **kept your fingers crossed**?

3. What do you **feel like** doing this weekend?

4. Where did you like to **hang out** when you were a kid? How about as a teenager?

5. Have you **checked out** any interesting new places lately? Where?

6. What is one of the most **awesome** cities you've ever visited?

7. When was the last time you felt like calling someone **a jerk**?

8. What is a job that pays big **bucks**?

9. Who is a person that **cracks you up**? Why?

10. When you were a kid, who were you **nuts about**?

11. Describe a good **buddy** of yours.

12. When was the last time you told someone that something was **no big deal**?

13. What kind of music do you think is **cool**?

14. What can you do for fun when you**'re broke**?

15. When was the last time someone told you that they were **kidding**?

cool

CHAPTER

2

no pain, no gain

a jock

give up

bug

classy

laid-back

go blank

show off

a nerd

never mind

can't stand

be beat

money to burn

kick back

fall for someone

Student Group 1

Learn the meanings of five expressions by completing the following exercises. Work with Student Group 1 or by yourself.

■ **GUESS** the meanings of the five expressions.

1) Pascal is a total jock. The only thing he likes to do is play sports.

2) Don't give up school now! You've only got two more weeks!

3) If you want to build your muscles, you have to work out regularly. No pain, no gain!

4) It really bugs me when I have to wait for a long time.

5) That little French boutique sells classy clothes.

■ **CHECK OUT** the definitions and examples of the expressions.

1) a jock—someone very dedicated to sports.
   He skis, windsurfs, mountain bikes, and plays soccer every week. What a jock!

2) give up—stop, quit trying, surrender.
   He tried to give up smoking several times, but he couldn't.

3) no pain, no gain—if you want something, you have to work for it.
   To become a doctor, you have to have a no pain, no gain attitude!

4) bug someone—bother, disturb, irritate, annoy.
   Steve bugs me because he talks too much about his work.

5) classy—high quality, elegant, stylish, sophisticated.
   Princess Diana was a very classy person.

■ **QUICK FIX**—Match the expressions to the words that are similar.

1) quit   ___classy

2) stylish   ___a jock

3) earn   ___bug

4) sports *freak*   ___give up

5) annoy   ___no pain, no gain

■ **CLOZE IT**—Use one of the above expressions to complete the sentences. Be sure to check your grammar!

1) Calling the bank_____me because I can't get a human voice on the line!

2) If you don't do your homework, you won't learn: _____!

3) Richard is_____football_____: He lives for the game!

4) Roses, champagne, chocolate. He's a _____guy.

5) English is difficult, but I'm not going to _____.

■ **SENSE OR NONSENSE**—With your classmates, discuss the sentences and decide if they do or don't make sense.

1) I don't know. I **give up.**_____

2) **Jocks** can talk about everything from sports to opera._____

3) *Getting stuck* in traffic when I'm already late doesn't **bug** me at all!_____

4) **No pain, no gain**! I didn't have to do anything._____

5) The Lexus is a **classy** car._____

■ **PLUG IT IN**—Use the expressions to replace the underlined words. Make sure to check your grammar! Check the Index/Glossary for words you may not know.

1) Leonardo has become a big soccer <u>fan</u>. That's all he wants to do nowadays!

2) James Bond, Agent 007, is a very <u>sophisticated</u> character.

3) It <u>gets on my nerves</u> when you start to tell me something but don't finish.

4) If you want to lose weight, you need to have a <u>stick-with-it</u> attitude.

5) Come on! Don't <u>quit</u> now! You can do it!

Student Group 2

Learn the meanings of the following five expressions by completing the exercises. Work with Student Group 2 or by yourself.

■ **GUESS** the meanings of the five expressions.

1) Henry is a **laid-back** guy. Nothing ever gets on his nerves.

2) I knew the answer, but I **went blank** when the teacher asked me.

3) Oscar loves to **show off** his muscles to the girls.

4) Bill Gates of Microsoft is a computer **nerd**.

5) Oh, **never mind**! I just remembered what I was looking for.

■ **CHECK OUT** the definitions and examples of the expressions.

1) **laid-back**— easy-going, relaxed, calm, mellow.
    Everyone likes my parents because they are so laid-back.

2) **go blank/draw a blank**—suddenly forget something.
    I just can't remember his name. I'm drawing a blank.

3) **show off**—try to get a lot of attention, brag.
    Abdul loves to show off his Ferrari.

4) **a nerd**—a person who is very smart, but often has strange social behavior, *weird*.
    Bob is a little difficult to work with because he's a nerd.

5) **never mind**—don't worry about it, forget it.
    Have you seen my sweater? Oh, I just found it. Never mind!

■ **QUICK FIX**—Match the expressions to the words that are similar.

1) peaceful   ___a nerd

2) can't remember ___go blank

3) forget it   ___show off

4) brag   ___never mind

5) a weirdo   ___laid-back

■ **CLOZE IT**—Use one of the above expressions to complete the sentences. Be sure to check your grammar!

1) I just_____! I don't know. Let me think.

2) Madonna loves to _____by doing wild things.

3) Scott plays computer games all day because he is such _____.

4) People who live near the beach can enjoy a _____lifestyle.

5) Seng: I forgot your book!   Ed: _____. I don't need it today.

■ **SENSE OR NONSENSE**—With your classmates, discuss the sentences and decide if they do or don't make sense.

1) Valerie is so **laid-back** that she's always complaining._____

2) It's really important, so **never mind**._____

3) Students never **go blank** when they have to answer a question._____

4) Gary is a great person to *go out with* because he is such **a nerd**._____

5) My neighbor makes big *bucks*, but he never **shows off** because he's so modest._____

■ **PLUG IT IN**—Use the expressions to replace the underlined words. Make sure to check your grammar! Check the Index/Glossary for words you may not know.

1) Brian loves to <u>brag about</u> his big new truck.

2) Long-haired surfer Sam is a very *mellow* person.

3) When I spilled coffee, she said <u>not to worry about it</u>.

4) What's that guy's name? I <u>can't remember</u>, but I know that I know!

5) It's good to be a little bit of a computer *freak* nowadays.

Student Group 3

Learn the meanings of the following five expressions by completing the exercises. Work with Student Group 3 or by yourself.

■ **GUESS** the meanings of the five expressions.

1) Yuck, I can't stand to eat liver!

2) I'm so beat that I can't stay awake another minute.

3) Maya must have money to burn because she sure spends a lot.

4) Let's kick back tonight and watch *the tube* (TV).

5) I'm falling for him. I feel happy and excited whenever he's around!

■ **CHECK OUT** the definitions and examples of the expressions.

1) can't stand—dislike, hate, detest, not tolerate.
   I can't stand people who lie.

2) be beat—be very tired, sleepy, exhausted.
   Larry worked 15 hours today, so he is beat!

3) money to burn—have extra money to spend.
   Let's go to Las Vegas. We've got money to burn!

4) kick back—relax, do very little.
   Work was slow this afternoon, so we kicked back.

5) fall for someone—begin to feel love for someone.
   Vincent is falling for Adriana. He just sent her a dozen long-stemmed red roses!

■ **QUICK FIX**—Match the expressions to the words that are similar.

1) love   ___kick back

2) hate   ___money to burn

3) spend   ___be beat

4) sleepy   ___fall for someone

5) do nothing   ___can't stand

■ **CLOZE IT**—Use one of the above expressions to complete the sentences. Be sure to check your grammar!

1) I don't *feel like* doing anything. I think I'm going to _____ for awhile.

2) Lee _____ her handsome Italian classmate.

3) I need to go home and sleep because I_____.

4) He's such *a jerk* , so I try not to think about him because I _____him.

5) Sally seems to wear a new dress every day. She must have_____.

■ **SENSE OR NONSENSE**—With your classmates, discuss the sentences and decide if they do or don't make sense.

1) He *bugs* me so much I **can't stand** him._____

2) I hate to **kick back** when I'm tired._____

3) I'm **falling for him** because he's so thoughtful and funny._____

4) Ted Turner, an executive with AOL Time Warner, has **money to burn.**_____

5) I'm so **beat** that I'm going to run 5 miles right now._____

■ **PLUG IT IN**—Use the expressions to replace the underlined words. Make sure to check your grammar! Check the Index/Glossary for words you may not know.

1) I wish I could buy that beautiful painting, but I don't have <u>any extra cash</u>.

2) Sasha <u>is starting to like</u> Asami more and more.

3) I'm <u>dead to the world</u>. Time for bed!

4) Let's <u>stay home</u> and watch a couple of movies.

5) My car broke down again! I <u>hate</u> it!

Questions to Ask Someone from Student Group 1

Ask Student 1 the following questions. He or she will tell you the answers. You should write down the answers. Student 1 can look at pages 20-21 to find the answers.

■ **TELL ME:** Ask Student 1 the following questions to get the expressions.

1) What is an expression which means you don't get something for nothing?____

2) What is a way to say stop trying something?_____

3) Is there a way to describe a person who only likes to do sports?_____

4) How can I describe someone or something that is very stylish?_____

5) What is a way to say that something bothers you?_____

■ **MAKE THIS MAKE SENSE:** Ask Student 1 to change these sentences to make sense.

1) It wouldn't **bug me** at all if you played loud rock-n-roll at 3:00 a.m. on Monday.

2) You should **give up** eating healthy food to get in great physical shape.

3) If you don't want to get more money, have a **no pain, no gain** attitude.

4) A Mercedes Benz is not a **classy** car.

5) Typical **jocks** are interested in literature, art, and music.

Questions to Ask Someone from Student Group 2

Ask Student 2 the following questions. He or she will tell you the answers. You should write down the answers. Student 2 can look at pages 22-23 to find the answers.

■ **TELL ME:** Ask Student 2 the following questions to get the expressions.

1) Is there a way to describe someone who loves to get attention?_____

2) What can you call someone who is smart but strange?_____

3) How can I say that I suddenly forgot what I was thinking about?_____

4) What is a way to say that someone is relaxed and peaceful?_____

5) Is there a way to say don't worry about what just happened?_____

■ **MAKE THIS MAKE SENSE:** Ask Student 2 to change these sentences to make sense.

1) Alex is a computer **nerd**. He never spends time on his computer.

2) I never **go blank**. That's why I can't remember her name!

3) **Never mind**. I really need your help.

4) Keiko is so modest and quiet. She's always **showing off**.

5) Bella is so **laid-back** that she always loses her temper.

Questions to Ask Someone from Student Group 3

Ask Student 3 the following questions. He or she will tell you the answers. You should write down the answers. Student 3 can look at pages 24-25 to find the answers.

■ **TELL ME:** Ask Student 3 following questions to get the expressions.

1) What is a way to say that I'm really tired?_____

2) What can I say if I think I love someone?_____

3) Is there another way to say I don't like something?_____

4) If I can spend as much money as I want, what can I say?_____

5) I don't feel like doing very much tonight. How can I express this?_____

■ **MAKE THIS MAKE SENSE:** Ask Student 3 to change these sentences to make sense.

1) I have so much **money to burn** that I can't go out for a fancy dinner.

2) I **can't stand** eating spinach, so let's have some for dinner.

3) Most men hate to **kick back** and watch sports.

4) Matty is so **beat** that she is going to go back to the office to work more.

5) Karim is **falling for** Karen because she is such a jerk.

Students 1—2—3

Before you begin the Halftime Activities, you must first complete pages 20-28 of Chapter 2. These activities are designed to get you to think about and discuss the meaning and use of the 15 expressions you have just studied.

■ **EXPRESSION GUIDE:** With your class, in small groups, or with friends, look over and talk about the idioms and slang you've been studying. Write down any extra information. Here are some questions to ask each other:

1) What kinds of people do you think use these expressions?
   (young, old, male, female...)

2) Where do you think you might hear these expressions?
   (school, beach, home, work, restaurant, nightclub, store...)

3) How do you think people say these expressions?
   (happy, angry, neutral, excited...)

EXPRESSION GUIDE

a jock *slang*	give up	no pain, no gain	bug	classy
laid-back *slang*	go blank	show off *slang*	a nerd *slang*	never mind
can't stand	be beat	money to burn	kick back	fall for someone

■ **CIRCLE AND DISCUSS** key words or phrases that show the meaning of the expression. It's best to work with a partner.

1) I think Earl is **falling for Christina**. He told me he wants to see her everyday.

2) Fred is nice, but he is **a science nerd**. He loves talking about it all the time!

3) I'm not going to **give up**. I've already worked too hard, and I'm almost finished.

4) That **bugs me** that Julie left five long messages on my answering machine without giving me a chance to call her back. It wasn't even an emergency!

5) Ryo must have **money to burn**. He treated his whole class to a sushi dinner!

6) Sorry, I just **went** totally **blank**! Give me a second to remember.

7) Gina is quite **a jock**. Even when there are people at her house, she wants to watch sports on TV.

8) Lou is a great snowboarder. I love to watch him **show off**. He can spin, jump, and fly!

9) Last weekend we just **kicked back** at home, read the paper, rented videos, and played cards and darts.

10) Dominique is one of the most **laid-back** people I've ever met. She is so cool, easy-going, and friendly.

11) Bellagio is the **classiest** new hotel casino in Las Vegas. It rivals Caesar's Palace.

12) Look at Brad! He's falling asleep standing up! He **must be** completely **beat**.

13) I worked everyday for four months straight to finish this book. **No pain, no gain** was my motto!

14) What was I going to . . . Oh **never mind**! I just remembered.

15) We **can't stand** anyone who hurts kids, the elderly, or animals.

■ **FIND OUT** about some grammar points and additional meanings of some expressions. Consult the Grammar Guide in Appendix E on page 181 for more information.

1) bug—We studied the verb phrase **bug someone**, which is transitive (has an object). However, **bug** as a noun usually refers to some type of insect. There are also two more very common idiomatic meanings:

   a) Marilyn caught **a bug** and has been sick all week.

   (a virus or bacteria that makes someone sick)

b) This computer game is fun, but it has too many **bugs** in it.

(errors, malfunctions)

Decide which meaning of **bug** is used in the sentence below:

c) A lot of students are absent because of the **bug** that is going around._____

2) beat—**Beat** also has many idiomatic meanings in English. Here are just two more common expressions:

a) It **beats me** why they left right before the game ended!

(I don't know. I have no idea.)

b) That store has great prices. They **can't be beat**!

(the best, wonderful, satisfying)

Complete the following sentence by using one of the meanings of **beat**:

c) The sushi at Nobu's_____!

3) fall for someone—While **fall for someone** means to start to love someone, if you **fall for something**, you are tricked or fooled! For example:

a) They told you that used car was worth $10,000? I can't believe you **fell for it**!

What do you think the sentence below means?

b) He is such a womanizer. I can't believe she fell for him! _____

4) nerd—The slang word **nerd** is also often used as an adjective: **nerdy**. In the sentence below, decide where to put a **nerd** (noun) or **nerdy** (adjective):

a) If I wear these old_____clothes to the party, everyone might think I'm a_____! I really need to go shopping.

5) show off—The idiom **show off** is a phrasal verb, but it can also become a noun: **a show-off**. In the sentence below, decide where to put **show off** as a verb or noun.

a) Fabio is _____. He_____ every chance he gets.

6) can't stand—The expression **can't stand** must be followed by a gerund or a noun. (see **feel like**, pg. 13). In the following sentences, decide whether the underlined words are a noun phrase or a gerund phrase.

a) He **can't stand** <u>being late</u>.   *b)* He **can't stand** <u>late people</u>.

■ **EXPRESSION LOG:** (1) Choose 10 expressions from this chapter to practice by writing original sentences, then (2) add two new expressions that you hear. Follow the New Expression Guide in Appendix A on page 159.

■ **LISTEN** and **WRITE**: 1) Write the expression in the box as you hear it being described, and then 2) decide whether the expression was used in a meaningful way. Circle Y for yes and N for no.

1. _____	2. _____	3. _____	4. _____	5. _____
_____	_____	_____	_____	_____
Y N	Y N	Y N	Y N	Y N
6. _____	7. _____	8. _____	9. _____	10. _____
_____	_____	_____	_____	_____
Y N	Y N	Y N	Y N	Y N
11. _____	12. _____	13. _____	14. _____	15. _____
_____	_____	_____	_____	_____
Y N	Y N	Y N	Y N	Y N

Rules:
Roll the die. If your number is:
- Odd (1, 3, 5), ask a question using an expression of your choice.
  Write your name in the box by the question mark: _____?
- Even (2, 4, 6), make a statement using an expression of your choice. Write
  your name in the box by the exclamation mark: _____!

You have 15 seconds to think of your question or statement. Each expression
may be used only one time!

go blank	money to burn	classy
_____?	_____?	_____?
_____!	_____!	_____!
a nerd	give up	can't stand
_____?	_____?	_____?
_____!	_____!	_____!
bug	fall for someone	a jock
_____?	_____?	_____?
_____!	_____!	_____!
show off	no pain, no gain	laid-back
_____?	_____?	_____?
_____!	_____!	_____!
never mind	be beat	kick back
_____?	_____?	_____?
_____!	_____!	_____!

be beat

3

be dressed to kill

Student Group 1

Learn the meanings of the following five expressions by completing the exercises. Work with Student Group 1 or by yourself.

■ **GUESS** the meanings of the five expressions.

1) Christophe is the biggest slob I've ever met. It looks like a tornado hit his room!

2) I didn't lock my bike, and someone ripped it off!

3) Let's get dressed to kill for that party!

4) You'd better get with it or you'll miss your deadline!

5) After 15 hours on a plane, I bet you're tired.

■ **CHECK OUT** the definitions and examples of the expressions.

1) a slob—a messy person.
   My roommate is such a slob. She never washes her dishes.

2) rip off—steal, rob, make someone pay too much.
   I paid too much for this car. I got ripped off.

3) be dressed to kill—wear fancy or beautiful clothes.
   Maria always gets a lot of attention from guys because she dresses to kill.

4) get with it—pay attention, concentrate, start.
   Yuji had better get with it or else he's going to fail the class.

5) I bet—I see, I understand, I can imagine, I guess.
   You won $2,000 in Las Vegas! I bet you were happy!

■ **QUICK FIX**—Match the expressions to the words that are similar.

1) rob   ___ be dressed to kill

2) I imagine   ___ get with it

3) do the work   ___ rip off

4) fashionable   ___a slob

5) not neat   ___I bet

■ **CLOZE IT**—Use one of the above expressions to complete the sentences. Be sure to check your grammar!

1) He looks so sharp in his new Italian suit. He_____.

2) Don't be surprised when you see Tammy's bathroom. She's _____.

3) What happened to my car stereo? Someone_____it_____.

4) I have to get this finished, so I'd better_____right now.

5) It's 7:00 and you haven't eaten all day? _____you're hungry.

■ **SENSE OR NONSENSE**—With your classmates, discuss the sentences and decide if they do or don't make sense.

1) I'm so pleased that someone **ripped off** my new computer and color printer._____

2) It can be difficult to live with someone who is **a slob**._____

3) **I bet** you'll be happy if your boyfriend *breaks up* with you._____

4) Top models are usually **dressed to kill**._____

5) If you don't **get with it** soon, you'll finish on time._____

■ **PLUG IT IN**—Use the expressions to replace the underlined words. Make sure to check your grammar! Check the Index/Glossary for words you may not know.

1) We really need to pay attention and focus because we have to finish today.

2) She put on her long silk black dress and high heels for the dinner party.

3) Can you believe they tried to steal all the money from that store?

4) If you're a messy person, you should get a house cleaner.

5) You're going to Bali on vacation? I guess you're happy about that!

Student Group 2

Learn the meanings of the following five expressions by completing the exercises. Work with Student Group 2 or by yourself.

■ **GUESS** the meanings of the five expressions.

1) There was a lot of **junk food** at the party.

2) It can be fun to **goof off** in class, but we have to study too.

3) Everybody has to work overtime because we're **swamped**.

4) You'd better study for the test or you might **blow it**.

5) Don't tease them anymore. **Cut it out!**

■ **CHECK OUT** the definitions and examples of the expressions.

1) **junk food**—snack food that isn't nutritious, like potato chips or candy.
   My favorite types of junk food are french fries and ice cream.

2) **goof around/off**—spend time doing nothing productive, playing around.
   We need to stop goofing off and get back to work.

3) **be swamped**—be extremely busy.
   I'm so swamped today. I don't think I'll be able to finish.

4) **blow it**—make a mistake, ruin, destroy, lose your chance.
   I was too nervous during the job interview. I'm sure I blew it.

5) **cut it out**—stop it!
   Quit bugging me. Cut it out! Now!

■ **QUICK FIX**—Match the expressions to the words that are similar.

1) Don't!   ___blow it

2) too much to do   ___junk food

3) have fun   ___cut it out

4) make a mistake   ___goof around

5) corn chips   ___be swamped

■ **CLOZE IT**—Use one of the above expressions to complete the sentences. Be sure to check your grammar!

1) Don't_____when you call her up to ask her out. Just be yourself.

2) Elizabeth _____so_____that she didn't have time to eat lunch.

3) Stop pulling your sister's hair! _____!

4) Sometimes it's good to _____on the computer to learn more.

5) Let's get some_____to snack on at the beach.

■ **SENSE OR NONSENSE**—With your classmates, discuss the sentences and decide if they do or don't make sense.

1) If you want to lose weight, don't eat **junk food**._____

2) **Cut it out!** I *can't stand* that._____

3) The meeting was a big success because you **blew it**._____

4) Tuyet is so **swamped** that she finished reading her novel._____

5) We had a great time on Saturday **goofing around** at the beach._____

■ **PLUG IT IN**—Use the expressions to replace the underlined words. Make sure to check your grammar! Check the Index/Glossary for words you may not know.

1) It's time to take final exams. That's why the students *are stressed out*.

2) Seth loves to munch on pretzels and M&Ms in the afternoon.

3) Don't bug me! I won't go if I don't want to.

4) I'm so happy my presentation is over and I didn't make any mistakes!

5) Let's go *hang out* downtown and see what's happening.

Student Group 3

Learn the meanings of the following five expressions by completing the exercises. Work with Student Group 3 or by yourself.

■ **GUESS** the meanings of the five expressions.

1) Carol is going to **fix me up with** Steve. Apparently he's a good guy.

2) I can't stand people who **put down** other people.

3) The president said that all the gossip about him and his private life is **bogus**.

4) Check out Jean-Marc *showing off* again. He **has such a big head**.

5) Flor has to **hit the books**, so she can't *go out* with us tonight.

■ **CHECK OUT** the definitions and examples of the expressions.

1) **fix someone up**—arrange a date or appointment for someone.
   Let me fix you up with my sister Saturday night.

2) **put down**—criticize, make other people seem stupid.
   John puts down other people because he is so insecure about himself.

3) **bogus**—not true, bad, unfair, not thoughtful, lame.
   Working overtime without earning more money is bogus.

4) **a big head**—too much self-importance.
   Don't give Dr. Lemper anymore compliments. He already has a big head.

5) **hit the books**—study.
   I never feel like hitting the books when the weather is so nice!

■ **QUICK FIX**—Match the expressions to the words that are similar.

1) false   ___put down

2) do homework   ___fix someone up

3) insult   ___a big head

4) egotistical   ___be bogus

5) get people together ___hit the books

■ **CLOZE IT**—Use one of the above expressions to complete the sentences. Be sure to check your grammar!

1) Su-Yeon and Chang are going to _____ to be ready for tomorrow's class.

2) Men with _____ think all the women want them.

3) Bruce is a really considerate person who never_____anyone_____.

4) He moved out and didn't even pay you the phone bill? That_____.

5) My friends_____with a really nice guy they work with.

■ **SENSE OR NONSENSE**—With your classmates, discuss the sentences and decide if they do or don't make sense.

1) Colin is a great student because he never **hits the books**._____

2) It's great to have a boss who is **bogus**._____

3) I feel comfortable with my boyfriend because he **puts me down**._____

4) Tiffany has such **a big head** that she thinks she can't do anything._____

5) Please don't **fix me up with** Mr. *Big Head*._____

■ **PLUG IT IN**—Use the expressions to replace the underlined words. Make sure to check your grammar! Check the Index/Glossary for words you may not know.

1) Ralph thinks he is God's gift to women. What <u>a big ego</u> he has!

2) Brad always <u>makes fun of</u> his little brother, but I think he is really jealous of him.

3) He was one hour late and didn't even say he was sorry. <u>That's lame</u>.

4) Mr. Park <u>arranged a meeting for us</u> with the head of his company.

5) Luke <u>studied</u> all weekend, so he is prepared for class Monday.

Questions to Ask Someone from Student Group 1

Ask Student 1 the following questions. He or she will tell you the answers. You should write down the answers. Student 1 can look at pages 36-37 to find the answers.

■ **TELL ME:** Ask Student 1 the following questions to get the expressions.

1) How do I describe someone who has great taste in clothes?_____

2) Is there an expression that means to pay attention and begin?_____

3) What is another way to say that you understand?_____

4) What can I say if I think I paid too much for something?_____

5) Is there a name for someone who never cleans anything?_____

■ **MAKE THIS MAKE SENSE**: Ask Student 1 to change these sentences to make sense.

1) I got **ripped off** when I paid $7.00 for this new CD.

2) You'd better **get with it** now, so go take a nap.

3) Young, single people don't usually get **dressed to kill** when they go out Saturday night.

4) Gustavo is such **a slob** because he always cleans his house.

5) **I bet** you're not upset about losing your job.

Questions to Ask Someone from Student Group 2

Ask Student 2 the following questions. He or she will tell you the answers. You should write down the answers. Student 2 can look at pages 38-39 to find the answers.

■ **TELL ME:** Ask Student 2 the following questions to get the expressions.

1) What can I say if I make a mistake?_____

2) How can I tell someone to stop bothering me?_____

3) Is there a way to say you are enjoying yourself doing "nothing"?_____

4) Is there a name for food that is fun to eat but not good for you?_____

5) How can I say that I'm totally busy?_____

■ **MAKE THIS MAKE SENSE:** Ask Student 2 to change these sentences to make sense.

1) I love it when you yell at me, so **cut it out!**

2) Let's get started on our final project by **goofing around**.

3) I'm so glad I **blew** my test.

4) She's so **swamped** that she's going to go to the movies.

5) I want to be healthy, so I'm going to eat more **junk food** from now on.

Questions to Ask Someone from Student Group 3

Ask Student 3 the following questions. He or she will tell you the answers. You should write down the answers. Student 3 can look at pages 40-41 to find the answers.

■ **TELL ME:** Ask Student 3 following questions to get the expressions.

1) What is a way to describe people who think they are better than others?_____

2) What do you say when one person criticizes another person?_____

3) How can I say I want my friend to introduce me to somebody?_____

4) Is there a way to say something is not fair or true?_____

5) How can I say that I really have to study?_____

■ **MAKE THIS MAKE SENSE:** Ask Student 3 to change these sentences to make sense.

1) It's fun to be **fixed up** with a jerk.

2) I need to **hit the books** because we don't have a test.

3) Jack is a very sincere person who has an incredibly **big head**.

4) I like to hang out with people who **put each other down** all the time.

5) It's **bogus** that my new car runs so well.

PART III It's Halftime

Students 1—2—3

Before you begin the Halftime Activities, you must first complete pages 36-44 of Chapter 3. These activities are designed to get you to think about and discuss the meaning and use of the 15 expressions you have just studied.

■ **EXPRESSION GUIDE:** With your class, in small groups, or with friends, look over and talk about the idioms and slang you've been studying. Write down any extra information. Here are some questions to ask each other:

1) What kinds of people do you think use these expressions?
   (young, old, male, female...)

2) Where do you think you might hear these expressions?
   (school, beach, home, work, restaurant, nightclub, store...)

3) How do you think people say these expressions?
   (happy, angry, neutral, excited...)

EXPRESSION GUIDE

fix someone up	put down	bogus *slang*	a big head	hit the books
a slob	rip off *slang*	be dressed to kill *slang*	get with it *slang*	I bet
junk food *slang*	goof off/around	be swamped	blow it *slang*	cut it out

■ **CIRCLE AND DISCUSS** key words or phrases that show the meaning of the expression. It's best to work with a partner!

1) Be careful of "get rich quick" offers you receive in the mail. They're usually **bogus**.

2) A lot of times tourists **get ripped off** because they don't know how things work and they end up paying too much for a lot of things they buy.

3) If you want to become an actor, you can't **blow it** when you audition! You won't get the part.

4) We **fixed Jody up** with our good friend Doug. They went out to dinner, but they didn't have a lot in common. Oh well, we tried!

5) If we want to win the next game, we'd better **get with it** and practice hard every day.

6) Sometimes I eat **junk food** in the afternoon when I have a lot of work to do, but I don't feel so great after I've eaten it.

7) Kids usually **put down** other kids who might be nerdy, funny looking, or not so smart.

8) You've worked every day this past month without one day off! **I bet you're beat!**

9) We're going to move into a new house next week, so **we're swamped**. We're too busy to go out!

10) Good lawyers always prepare for their cases. They often **hit the books** and lose sleep to get ready for court.

11) Andy knows he's **a slob**. That's why he never invites anyone to his house because he is embarrassed at how messy it is.

12) Stop tickling me! **Cut it out**! I can't breathe!

13) Ever since Trudy became the boss, she's gotten **a big head**. She thinks we should kiss the ground she walks on!

14) Wow! Cindy is **dressed to kill** tonight. I hope her boyfriend isn't the jealous type because she's going to get a lot of attention.

15) The students are **goofing around** again in the computer lab! They're not doing their work. They're surfing the net and reading their e-mail.

■ **FIND OUT** about some grammar points and additional meanings of some expressions. Consult the Grammar Guide in Appendix E on page 181 for more information.

1) **junk food**—The word **junk** in English basically means cheap, not good, or worthless. That is why **junk food** is used to describe food that isn't nutritious. Look at some other common expressions using the word **junk**. What do you think they mean?

    a) I get so much **junk mail** every day. What a waste of paper!_____

    b) I can't stand my car! What a **piece of junk**!_____

    c) I have too much **junk**. I need to give it away or throw it out!_____

2) **get with it**—The verb **get** is highly idiomatic in English. Here are just two more common uses of **get**. Read the sentences below and decide which one means "understand" and which one means "able to".

    a) I'm so happy that we **get** to go skiing this winter. _____

    b) Everyone laughed but me, because I didn't **get** the joke. _____

3) **blow it**—The verb **blow** is also very idiomatic in English. Below are two more common expressions. Which one do you think means "lose your temper" and which one means "waste money"?

    a) He is going to **blow up** when he finds out that you crashed his car._____

    b) He **blew** his whole paycheck at the bar._____

4) **I bet**—You've learned what **I bet** means. What do you think **You bet** means? Read the sentences below and take a guess.

    a) **You bet** I can help you move. When do you want me to come over?_____

    b) Jim: Thanks a lot!   Tom: **You bet**!_____

5) **put down**—You studied that to **put someone down** means to criticize or insult someone, but if you **put something down**, it simply means to place something somewhere. Notice that **put down** is a separable transitive phrasal verb. You can also use **put down** as a noun, as in a **put-down**, which is an insult. Use a form of **put down** to make sentences below:

    a) Be careful with that glass. You'll break it! _____

    b) Wow, he called me a nerd. That's_____

6) **fix up**—The word **fix** also has many idiomatic meanings. You learned that you can **fix somebody up with someone**, which means to arrange a date or an appointment for someone. You can also **fix somebody up with something**, which means to arrange for someone to get or receive something. In the general sense, **fix** simply means to repair something. Read the sentences below and decide what **fix** means.

    a) Mr. Tanaka told me that the company would **fix me up with a car**._____

    b) Gary **fixed** my VCR. Now I can record some movies._____

7) **rip off**—The slang expression **rip off** has some important grammar uses. As a phrasal **verb**, it is always transitive (separable—has an object). Because it is transitive, it can be (1) active or (2) passive. Finally, **rip off** can also be a (3) noun. Look at **rip off** in the following sentences and choose (1) (2) or (3) to describe the grammar use.

a) That movie was **a rip-off**! Don't waste your money on it. _____

b) Be careful in that store! They'll **rip you off** if you don't bargain. _____

c) I **got ripped off when** I bought that stupid car. _____

■ **EXPRESSION LOG:** (1) Choose 10 expressions from this chapter to practice by writing original sentences, then (2) add two new expressions that you hear. Follow the New Expression Guide in Appendix A on page 159.

Listen to the stories. As you hear them being described, number the expressions #1—#15. Write down any key words you hear that help you

blow it #____ *Key Words:*	**bogus** #____ *Key Words:*	**get with it** #____ *Key Words:*
swamped #____ *Key Words:*	**put down** #____ *Key Words:*	**I bet** #____ *Key Words:*
junk food #____ *Key Words:*	**a big head** #____ *Key Words:*	**cut it out** #____ *Key Words:*
goof off #____ *Key Words:*	**fix someone up** #____ *Key Words:*	**a slob** #____ *Key Words:*
hit the books #____ *Key Words:*	**dressed to kill** #____ *Key Words:*	**rip off** #____ *Key Words:*

RULES:
1) Roll the die. If your number is:
   - odd (1, 3, 5) you must choose an expression and say something false F_____
   - even (2, 4, 6) you must choose an expression and say something true T_____
2) Write your name by the T for True or the F for False. Use each expression only once.

cut it out	rip off	hit the books	a big head	fix someone up
T_____	T_____	T_____	T_____	T_____
F_____	F_____	F_____	F_____	F_____
swamped	a slob	junk food	blow it	I bet
T_____	T_____	T_____	T_____	T_____
F_____	F_____	F_____	F_____	F_____
put down	bogus	goof off	dressed to kill	get with it
T_____	T_____	T_____	T_____	T_____
F_____	F_____	F_____	F_____	F_____

Tic-Tac-Toe

Rules: Student X and Student O choose the expression they would like to use to make a correct and meaningful sentence. They have 20 seconds to make the sentence. The Student Referee will keep time, judge if the sentences are appropriate, and mark the selected boxes with X or O. The first student to get three in a row wins the game! Work with one or two classmates.

1.

blow it	laid-back	grab a bite
nerd	get with it	junk food
crack-up	go blank	swamped

2.

bogus	slob	kick back
jock	rip off	no pain, no gain
hit the books	bucks	cut it out

Dialogue Match

<u>Partner A:</u> Read over your part of the dialogue, and then begin the dialogue by reading the first line to Partner B. Partner B will listen to you and read another line of dialogue to you. You have to find the best line to read back to Partner B. Number your lines in the order that you read them (1, 3, 5, 7, 9, 11).

_____   What do you **feel like** doing this weekend?

_____   Yeah, I thought he was a **classy** guy too. I was **nuts about him** until I realized he was trying to make me jealous.

_____   That's true, I do, but you-know-who, Mr. **Big Head** might be there, and I don't **feel like** running into him.

_____   We could do that, but I don't want to **hang out** in a club all night.

_____   Neither can I. As soon as I noticed he **was putting me down**, I had to stop seeing him. That really **bugs me** when guys do that.

_____   It's **no big deal**. I just can't believe I **fell for him**!

Partner B: Read over your part of the dialogue. Then listen to Partner A read the first line of the dialogue to you. You have to look at your choices and read the line that best responds to Partner A's line. Partner A will then read another line to you. Number your lines in the order that you read them (2, 4, 6, 8, 10, 12).

____ I know, I thought he was a pretty **classy** guy, otherwise I would have never fixed you up with him in the first place.

____ Let me think. How about if we go **check out** that new salsa club downtown?

____ That's too bad. Oh well, let's **keep our fingers crossed** that the next guy will be better!

____ You're **kidding**! I thought you loved **getting dressed to kill** and **showing off** what an **awesome** salsa dancer you are!

____ That is so weird he was trying to make you feel jealous! I **can't stand** guys like that!

____ Oh, **I bet**. I'm sorry I **fixed you up with him**. He's a nice guy to work with, but I didn't know he could be such **a jerk**.

Shout It Out!

In groups of three, take turns (1) reading the sentences out loud, (2) shouting out a corresponding expression, and (3) using the expression in a sentence. Try to use as many expressions as possible! Write your sentences down. Be sure to look over the expressions you've been studying.

Example:

Student 1—Read: I'm totally wiped out! We've been moving boxes all day long. I have zero energy!

Student 2—Shout: **You're beat**!

Student 3—Respond: If **you're beat**, you should **kick back** tonight.

1) *Student 1*—Read: I really need to stop smoking. I've been coughing a lot lately and can't run as fast as I used to.

   Student 2—Shout:_____

   Student 3—Respond:_____

2) *Student 1*—Read: Whenever I have to speak in front of other people, I always forget what I was going to say!

Student 2—Shout:_____

Student 3—Respond:_____

3) *Student 1*—Read: That is really great about your new job. It sounds like a neat place to work. It's a super career move.

Student 2—Shout:_____

Student 3—Respond:_____

4) *Student 1*—Read: We had a fun time Wednesday afternoon at work. We finished our work early, so we just sat around, ate some junk food, joked with each other and surfed the net.

Student 2—Shout:_____

Student 3—Respond:_____

5) *Student 1*—Read: My grandparents gave me $1,000 for my graduation gift. They told me to go have fun with it!

Student 2—Shout:_____

Student 3—Respond:_____

6) *Student 1*—Read: I can't do anything until I get my next paycheck! It's really hard to pay my bills and live paycheck to paycheck!

Student 2—Shout:_____

Student 3—Respond:_____

Grand Finale

Work with one or two partners to write a dialogue or a story using a minimum of 20 expressions from Chapters 1-2-3 and from your Expression Logs. There is no maximum, so use as many expressions as possible! Your teacher may announce winners!

be swamped

4

a backseat driver

a sweet tooth

down-to-earth

get over

look forward to

get together

in hot water

hang on

see someone

a blind date

go through

open-minded

make good time

give/have/take a shot

in the same boat

Student Group 1

Learn the meanings of the following five expressions by completing the exercises. Work with Student Group 1 or by yourself.

■ **GUESS** the meanings of the five expressions.

1) I didn't finish the homework either. We're **in the same boat**.

2) Keiko is **looking forward to** starting her new job.

3) Hey, I know how to drive! Don't be **a backseat driver**.

4) It took Pamela a month to **get over** her cold.

5) Gary can *hang out* with anyone because he is so **down-to-earth**.

■ **CHECK OUT** the definitions and examples of the expressions.

1) **in the same boat**—people who have the same trouble or problem.
   Scott: I need to get my car fixed again!
   Brian: I know what you mean buddy. *I'm in the same boat. I just spent $500.00 on a new transmission.*

2) **look forward to**—feel excited about something that you expect to happen or do.
   In general, most people look forward to the weekend.

3) **a backseat driver**—a person who tells the driver how to drive.
   Janice makes me nervous when I drive because she's such a backseat driver.

4) **get over**—recover, feel better.
   Arzu doesn't want to date anyone because she is still getting over her broken heart.

5) **down-to-earth**—easygoing, friendly, natural.
   Most people feel comfortable with Aline because she is so down-to-earth.

■ **QUICK FIX**—Match the expressions to the words that are similar.

1) glad about   ___down-to-earth

2) mellow   ___a backseat driver

3) heal   ___in the same boat

4) nervous passenger ___look forward to

5) similar difficulty ___get over

■ **CLOZE IT**—Use one of the above expressions to complete the sentences. Be sure to check your grammar.

1) She needs more time to_____the loss of her friend.

2) I'm_____ winter because I want to go skiing.

3) We're_____with this assignment we have to finish.

4) Annette is a very _____person you can talk to anytime about anything.

5) Ever since his car accident, he has become_____.

■ **SENSE OR NONSENSE**—With your classmates, discuss the sentences and decide if they do or don't make sense.

1) *Jerks* are usually **down-to-earth** people._____

2) If you're **in the same boat**, you can sometimes help each other._____

3) It's fun to drive across the country with **backseat drivers**._____

4) It takes about two weeks to **get over** the flu._____

5) I'm not **looking forward to** seeing a great concert Saturday night._____

■ **PLUG IT IN**—Use the expressions to replace the underlined words. Make sure to check your grammar! Check the Index/Glossary for words you may not know.

1) When are you coming to visit? We <u>can't wait to see you</u>!

2) I love my Grandpa because he is so <u>pleasant</u> with everyone.

3) Sofia is <u>in the exact same position</u> as Marine. They should talk about what to do.

4) Harry is still <u>recovering from</u> losing his job due to *lay-offs*.

5) I don't know what is worse: *a Sunday driver* or <u>someone who tells you how to drive</u>.

Student Group 2

Learn the meanings of the following five expressions by completing the exercises. Work with Student Group 2 or by yourself.

■ **GUESS** the meanings of the five expressions.

1) She doesn't want to date me because she's already seeing someone.

2) This was really fun. We should get together again sometime.

3) Oh, I'm in hot water. I forgot to call him back again!

4) *Yum*, banana cream pie. This will satisfy my sweet tooth.

5) Hang on five more minutes. We're almost there.

■ **CHECK OUT** the definitions and examples of the expressions.

1) see someone—date someone, *get to know* someone romantically, *go out*.
   We're starting to see each other more and more, at least three times a week now.

2) get together—spend time together socially, *hang out*.
   I love to get together with friends after work, especially on Friday night.

3) in hot water—be in some trouble
   Gustavo is in hot water with the teacher because he's always late to class.
   He thinks checking his e-mail is a good excuse, but he always interrupts us.

4) a sweet tooth—like to eat candy, desserts
   Sarah always has a sweet tooth for ice cream even if it is freezing cold outside.

5) hang on—wait, don't be impatient
   I hate hanging on the telephone waiting to talk to someone.

■ **QUICK FIX**—Match the expressions to the words that are similar.

1) problems   ___hang on

2) socialize   ___see someone

3) get close to someone ___get together

4) don't give up   ___ a sweet tooth

5) sugar   ___in hot water

■ **CLOZE IT**—Use one of the above expressions to complete the sentences. Be sure to check your grammar!

1) Every afternoon, I have such _____ that I almost always eat chocolate.

2) It will be fun to_____and go out for some sushi.

3) Don't worry, we won't be late. _____a few more minutes.

4) George let me borrow his car and I accidentally dented it. I'm _____now!

5) They've been _____regularly for the past five months. It's getting serious.

■ **SENSE OR NONSENSE**—With your classmates, discuss the sentences and decide if they do or don't make sense.

1) It's great to be **in hot water**._____

2) If you **see someone** a lot, maybe you're *falling for that person*._____

3) Verna's favorite **sweet tooth** "fix" is pizza._____

4) Impatient people can **hang on** easily._____

5) Students usually like to **get together** after class and go somewhere._____

■ **PLUG IT IN**—Use the expressions to replace the underlined words. Make sure to check your grammar! Check the Index/Glossary for words you may not know.

1) Do you like sugar or do you go for salty snacks?

2) They dated each other for two years before they got married.

3) Pascal is in for it now. Not only did he forget her birthday, he forgot Valentine's Day again too.

4) Some people say they would like to socialize, but they never do.

5) Would you please wait a few more days? We need a little more time.

Student Group 3

Learn the meanings of the following five expressions by completing the exercises. Work with Student Group 3 or by yourself.

■ **GUESS** the meanings of the five expressions.

1) I'm really nervous about this **blind date**. I hope I have a good time.

2) You have to **go through** the whole course to get the degree.

3) It is important to be **open-minded** when you visit other countries.

4) We **made great time** when we drove back to San Diego from Los Angeles.

5) I've never gone skydiving before, but I'll **give it a shot**.

■ **CHECK OUT** the definitions and examples of the expressions.

1) **blind date**—go out with someone you've never met before usually because your friends *fix you up*.
   *I just had the worst **blind date**! We had nothing to talk about.*

2) **go through**—experience something, finish.
   *I can't believe we **went through** all that bread already! Time for the store again!*

3) **open-minded**—tolerant, consider different ideas
   *Dale isn't **open-minded** when it comes to trying new food. He is a "meat and pota-toes" type of guy.*

4) **make good time**—get somewhere faster or finish something sooner than expected.
   *There is no traffic now, so we'll **make good time**.*

5) **give/have/take a shot**—a try, a possibility, take a chance. With the pronoun *it*, we say, "Give it a shot."
   *Mike **has** a **shot at** getting a better job, so he should go for it.*

■ **QUICK FIX**—Match the expressions to the words that are similar.

1) get somewhere quickly   ___a shot

2) a chance   ___blind date

3) social activity with unknown person   ___go through

4) not judgmental   ___open-minded

5) experience   ___make good time

■ **CLOZE IT**—Use one of the above expressions to complete the sentences. Be sure to check your grammar.

1) Every year, Claudia takes_____at winning the lottery to get a green card to emigrate to the United States.

2) It is difficult to travel with someone who isn't_____.

3) It took you only five hours! You really_____.

4) Philippe had to _____five interviews before he got the job.

5) My friends were really right about Steve. We had a great_____.

■ **SENSE OR NONSENSE**—With your classmates, discuss the sentences and decide if they do or don't make sense.

1) I love **making good time** in the morning getting to work._____

2) **Open-minded** people don't usually like foreign movies._____

3) **Blind dates** can be a waste of time._____

4) When you learn a new language, you really have to **give speaking a shot.**_____

5) A divorce is usually very easy to **go through.**_____

■ **PLUG IT IN**—Use the expressions to replace the underlined words. Make sure to check your grammar! Check the Index/Glossary for words you may not know.

1) I wanted to try surfing, so I signed up for lessons with a pro surfer.

2) We drove from Las Vegas to San Diego in five hours. We got there so fast.

3) Yoshi wants to completely finish this language program.

4) It is always good to work with objective and non-biased people.

5) Meeting a new person I've never seen before can be exciting.

Questions to Ask Someone from Student Group 1

Ask Student 1 the following questions. He or she will tell you the answers. You should write down the answers. Student 1 can look at pages 56-57 to find the answers.

■ **TELL ME:** Ask Student 1 the following questions to get the expressions.

1) Is there a way to say we share a similar experience?_____

2) What is a way to say get better?_____

3) Is there another way to say someone is friendly and easy-going?_____

4) How can I express that I feel happy about something I'm going to do?_____

5) What do you call someone who feels nervous in a car?_____

■ **MAKE THIS MAKE SENSE:** Ask Student 1 to change these sentences to make sense.

1) I'm **looking forward** to getting sick again this year.

2) I enjoy having **a backseat driver** tell me how to drive.

3) It's easy to **get over** a broken heart.

4) I don't know how you feel at all because we're **in the same boat.**

5) **Down-to-earth** people make me nervous.

Questions to Ask Someone from Student Group 2

Ask Student 2 the following questions. He or she will tell you the answers. You should write down the answers. Student 2 can look at pages 58-59 to find the answers.

■ **TELL ME:** Ask Student 2 the following questions to get the expressions.

1) How can I invite someone to do something?_____

2) What is another way to say WAIT?_____

3) Is there an expression to describe someone who likes sugar?_____

4) How can I say I'm in some trouble?_____

5) What is a way to say you go out with someone regularly?_____

■ **MAKE THIS MAKE SENSE:** Ask Student 2 to change these sentences to make sense.

1) I don't mind **hanging on** the telephone waiting for someone to answer.

2) I have **a sweet tooth**; I love to eat potato chips.

3) I enjoy **getting together** with people who are jerks.

4) It's not fun to **see someone** you really like a lot.

5) I won't get **in hot water** if I crash my friend's car.

Questions to Ask Someone from Student Group 3

Ask Student 3 the following questions. He or she will tell you the answers. You should write down the answers. Student 3 can look at pages 60-61 to find the answers.

■ **TELL ME:** Ask Student 3 following questions to get the expressions.

1) How can you say you got somewhere really fast?_____

2) Is there a way to say you finished using something?_____

3) How can you say you're going out with someone you've never met?_____

4) What is a way to say you can appreciate different ideas?_____

5) Is there a way to say to try something?_____

■ **MAKE THIS MAKE SENSE:** Ask Student 1 to change these sentences to make sense.

1) It is difficult to discuss anything with **open-minded** people.

2) It's not easy to **go through** ice cream.

3) OK, I'll **give it a shot**. I won't try it!

4) **A blind date** is the only way to meet somebody.

5) We **make good time** getting to school in the heavy morning traffic.

Students 1—2—3

Before you begin the Halftime Activities, you must first complete pages 56-64 of Chapter 4. These activities are designed to get you to think about and discuss the meaning and use of the 15 expressions you have just studied.

■ **EXPRESSION GUIDE:** With your class, in small groups, or with friends, look over and talk about the idioms and slang you've been studying. Write down any extra information. Here are some questions to ask each other:

1) What kinds of people do you think use these expressions?
   (young, old, male, female...)

2) Where do you think you might hear these expressions?
   (school, beach, home, work, restaurant, nightclub, store...)

3) How do you think people say these expressions?
   (happy, angry, neutral, excited...)

EXPRESSION GUIDE

in the same boat	look forward to	a backseat driver	get over	down-to-earth
see someone	get together	in hot water	a sweet tooth	hang on
a blind date	go through	open-minded	make good time	give/have/take a shot

■ **CIRCLE AND DISCUSS** key words or phrases that show the meaning of the expression. Be sure to work with a partner!

1) Reggie, my puppy, is **in hot water** again. Yesterday he chewed up the patio furniture. And today he broke the screen door. I'm taking him to dog obedience school!

2) I want you to meet my friend Takae. I like hanging out with her because she's so **down-to-earth**. No matter what we do, I always feel comfortable with her. You will too.

3) Claudia **went through** a lot of trouble at the airport because they lost her luggage. First, she had to wait to fill out a form. Then they asked her to claim

her luggage, but it wasn't hers. Finally, she got it . . . two weeks later!

4) We're definitely **looking forward to** the end of school because we have a month break! We're going to visit the Grand Canyon, Zion National Park, and Bryce Canyon.

5) I'm so happy I **made good time** cleaning up my house. I finished before I thought I would, so now I can kick back and relax!

6) Pri wants to continue studying here, and so do I. She doesn't have enough money, and neither do I. She needs to get a job somewhere, and I do too. I'm **in the same boat** as she is.

7) When I get a **sweet tooth**, my first choice is a big fat chewy chocolate chip cookie with walnuts. If I can't find a good cookie, I usually *settle* for some M&Ms.

8) I'm going to apply for the job even though I don't have all the experience they require. I do have some experience, so I might as well **give it a shot**!

9) We've been **seeing each other** for about three months now, but we still haven't said "I love you."

10) It took Chris two months to **get over** most of the injuries from his horrible car accident and one full year to completely recover.

11) Liz said she was really nervous before her **blind date** with Matthew. Their friends had told them a lot about each other, but they had never seen each other before.

12) Our supervisor told us that he didn't know why we didn't get a pay raise when everyone else did. He asked us to **hang on** for two more weeks so he could find out why.

13) I'm sorry I've become **a backseat driver**. I'm not used to so much traffic. I don't mean to make you nervous when you drive. I'll just shut my eyes!

14) We should definitely keep in touch and **get together** whenever you come back here to visit. Just let me know when you're coming.

15) Diego is going to be a great international business lawyer because he is very smart, easy to get along with, and **open-minded**.

■ **FIND OUT** about some grammar points and additional meanings of some expressions. Consult the Grammar Guide in Appendix E on page 181 for more information.

1) see someone—The verb **see** can be stative or nonstative, and it has many idiomatic meanings. Remember, a stative verb is not usually used in the

progressive. In addition to **see** meaning to date someone, here are three more common uses of **see**. Match the sentences to their meanings.

a)	Look! You can see the planet Venus tonight.___	*1)*	appointment (nonstative)
b)	I'm seeing the dentist at 12:00 on Monday.___	*2)*	understand (stative)
c)	Do you see what I mean?___	*3)*	go out (nonstative)
d)	We started seeing each other last summer.___	*4)*	view (stative)

2) **look forward to**—This expression is followed by a gerund or noun phrase. In the sentences below, decide if the underlined phrase is a gerund or noun.

   a) He's looking forward to <u>visiting us next year</u>.   _____

   b) She's looking forward to <u>school</u>.   _____

   c) I'm looking forward to <u>shopping</u>.   _____

3) **get together**—This expression can be used as a verb, a noun or even a gerund! Look at the following sentences and see if you can tell which is which.

   a) Lisa is having a get together next Saturday night.   _____

   b) Annette and I are getting together for coffee later at Cafe Lulu.

   _____

   c) He enjoys getting together with the guys and watching the ballgame.

   _____

4) **a backseat driver**—Another type of annoying person in a car is **a Sunday driver**. While **a backseat driver** is a passenger, **a Sunday driver** is driving the car. Read the sentence below and write a definition for **a Sunday driver**.

   a) Just my luck! Whenever I'm in a rush, I always get stuck behind **a Sunday driver**. Now I'm going to be really late!

   Definition:_____

5) **hang on**—There are two other common expressions which are synonyms to **hang on**. The first is **hold on**, which means to wait. Both **hang on** and **hold on** are frequently used on the telephone. The second common expression is **hang in there**, which means don't give up or quit. It is similar to **hang on** because it also signifies don't be impatient. Read the situation below and offer some advice. Explain what your advice means.

   a) I'm really *beat* because I have had my *folks* visiting for a month! They're leaving in two more weeks. I love them but . . .

   Advice and explanation:_____

6) **open-minded, make good time**—These two expressions have "twin expressions" with the opposite meaning: **closed-minded** and **make bad time**. Read the two sentences below and fill the blank with one of the four expressions:

   a) It took us five hours to go 50 miles! We made_____time!

   b) Don't ask for his opinion about politics. He's very _____minded.

a blind date

■ **LISTEN** and **WRITE:**

1) Listen to each sentence and write down the expression you hear.

2) Decide whether or not the sentence is logical.

3) Explain why the expression was or was not used in a meaningful way.

Expression	Logical yes or no	Explanation
1.		
2.		
3.		
4.		
5.		
6.		
7.		
8.		
9.		
10.		
11.		
12.		
13.		
14.		
15.		

RULES:
1) Roll the die. If your number is:
   - Odd (1, 3, 5), choose an expression and use it in the negative.
     Then write your name in the box by the negative: _____ -
   - Even (2, 4, 6), choose an expression and use it in the affirmative.
     Then write your name in the box by the affirmative: _____ +
2) You have 15 seconds to think of your negative or affirmative phrase.
   Each expression may be used only one time!

get together _____ - _____ +	**open-minded** _____ - _____ +	**make good time** _____ - _____ +
a sweet tooth _____ - _____ +	**down-to-earth** _____ - _____ +	**in the same boat** _____ - _____ +
look forward to _____ - _____ +	**in hot water** _____ - _____ +	**a backseat driver** _____ - _____ +
see someone _____ - _____ +	**go through** _____ - _____ +	**hang on** _____ - _____ +
a blind date _____ - _____ +	**give it a shot** _____ - _____ +	**get over** _____ - _____ +

a morning/night person

a hunk

talk someone's ears off

come in handy

get along

Long time no see.

ring a bell

come/go over

figure out

have/get it together

pushy

a lemon

break up

get in shape

on someone's back

Work It Out

Student Group 1

Learn the meanings of the following five expressions by completing the exercises. Work with Student Group 1 or by yourself.

■ **GUESS** the meanings of the five expressions.

1) A lot of women think Brad Pitt is **a hunk**.

2) Julie **talked my ears off** about her new boyfriend.

3) Let's bring all the maps. I'm sure they'll **come in handy**.

4) I love my job. All of the employees are nice and everyone **gets along** great.

5) **Long time no see**! How have you been doing?

■ **CHECK OUT** the definitions and examples of the expressions.

1) **a hunk**—a handsome and well-built man.
   *Have you seen Cindy's new boyfriend? He's **a hunk**. No wonder she's so happy!*

2) **talk someone's ears off**—talk way too much about something to someone.
   *The media **has talked everyone's ears off** about the president's personal life.*

3) **come in handy**—something that is useful.
   *I always carry my Swiss Army Knife because I never know when it may **come in handy**.*

4) **get along**—live or work together in a friendly and comfortable way, be compatible.
   *My brother and I **didn't get along** when we were kids, but we do now.*

5) **Long time no see**—a greeting used when people haven't seen each other for awhile
   *Wow! I can't believe it! HOW ARE YOU? **Long time no see!***

■ **QUICK FIX**—Match the expressions to the words that are similar.

1) helpful   ___a hunk

2) gorgeous guy   ___long time no see

3) feel good with someone   ___talk someone's ears off

4) missed you   ___get along

5) overly talkative   ___come in handy

■ **CLOZE IT**—Use one of the expressions to complete the sentences. Be sure to check your grammar!

1) My mom_____about what my sister did.

2) Not only is he sweet, but he's also tall, dark, and handsome. What_____!

3) Look who's here! What a surprise! _____!

4) I'm really comfortable with my new roommate. We_____well.

5) I love my new computer. It_____for doing so many things.

■ **SENSE OR NONSENSE**—With your classmates, discuss the sentences and decide if they do or don't make sense.

1) I never get a chance to speak when he **talks my ears off** about his work._____

2) I just saw you yesterday. Hey—**long time no see**._____

3) Mel Gibson is a **hunk**._____

4) We **get along** so well that I think we'll take a trip together._____

5) I don't need this tape recorder because it **comes in handy**._____

■ **PLUG IT IN**—Use the expressions to replace the underlined words. Make sure to check your grammar! Check the Index/Glossary for words you may not know.

1) It has been years since we saw each other. You haven't changed a bit!

2) Bill is so difficult to work with because he doesn't try to please anyone.

3) Richard can't stop discussing football with us!

4) He may be good-looking and muscular, but he is also *a jerk*.

5) You should buy your own washer and dryer. Having your own is so convenient.

Student Group 2

Learn the meanings of the following five expressions by completing the exercises. Work with Student Group 2 or by yourself.

■ **GUESS** the meanings of the five expressions.

1) Do you remember now? Does that **ring a bell**?

2) How about if we **come over** at 7:00?

3) I get most of my work done early because I'm **a morning person**.

4) Mizuki has to **figure out** which classes to take.

5) Karen is young, but she has really **got it together**.

■ **CHECK OUT** the definitions and examples of the expressions.

1) **to ring a bell**—be familiar, be able to remember.
   His name doesn't ring a bell, but his face does.

2) **come/go over**—visit, drop by someone's house.
   Come over anytime! You're always welcome.
   Mi casa es tu casa! (my house is your house—Spanish)

3) **a morning/night person**—someone who is most alert or energetic early or late.
   Are you a morning person or a night person?

4) **figure out**—solve, understand
   I need to figure out how to set up my new surround sound stereo.

5) **have/get it together**—be healthy emotionally and mentally, have control of your life
   Scott needs to get it together and figure out his money problems.

■ **QUICK FIX**—Match the expressions to the words that are similar.

1)	visit	___have it together
2)	be productive at a certain time	___ring a bell
3)	stable	___a morning/night person
4)	heard before	___come over
5)	calculate	___figure out

■ **CLOZE IT**—Use one of the above expressions to complete the sentences. Be sure to check you grammar!

1) I want to_____how to use my new software application.

2) Don't talk to Chris when he wakes up. He's definitely not_____.

3) Kim really _____when it comes to being a master teacher.

4) This place has changed so much. Nothing _____even though I used to live here!

5) I'm sorry, but you really ought to call before you _____.

■ **SENSE OR NONSENSE**—With your classmates, discuss the sentences and decide if they do or don't make sense.

1) Oh, that **rings a bell**! I just went blank._____

2) I usually go to bed around 3:00 a.m. because I'm **a night person**._____

3) It's OK to **come over** at 5:00 in the morning, especially on Sunday._____

4) Henry Ford really **had it together** as a businessman._____

5) Einstein **figured out** the Theory of Relativity._____

■ **PLUG IT IN**—Use the expressions to replace the underlined words. Make sure to check your grammar! Check the Index/Glossary for words you may not know.

1) Keiko is taking charge of her life. She has a great new job and a great new home.

2) David is so happy that he solved the computer network problems.

3) I don't think I've ever seen this before. I'm sorry I can't help you out.

4) Steve usually gets up at 4:30 a.m. and starts working. He's an early bird.

5) My aunt and uncle sometimes pop in on a Saturday afternoon to say hello.

Student Group 3

Learn the meanings of the following five expressions by completing the exercises. Work with Student Group 3 or by yourself.

■ **GUESS** the meanings of the five expressions.

1) That car salesman **is very pushy.** Be sure to take your time!

2) No one will buy this car! It's **a lemon.**

3) I **broke up** with my boyfriend when I found out he was seeing someone else.

4) It's time to **get in shape**! I'm joining a health club.

5) My teacher is **on my back** about not doing my homework.

■ **CHECK OUT** the definitions and examples of the expressions.

1) **pushy**—aggressive, bossy.
   *That guy is too **pushy**. I don't want to go out with him.*

2) **a lemon**—a faulty appliance, usually a car.
   *Before you buy the car, you'd better take it to a mechanic to have it checked out to make sure it's not **a lemon**.*

3) **break up**—end a relationship, usually with a boyfriend or girlfriend.
   *Robert decided to **break up** with his girlfriend because he didn't feel that serious about her.*

4) **get in shape**—take care of oneself physically, usually through exercise.
   *Elena wants to **get in shape** before "bikini season".*

5) **on someone's back**—bug, bother, or put pressure on someone.
   *My parents are **on my back** about getting married.*

■ **QUICK FIX**—Match the expressions to the words that are similar.

1) bad car   ___break up

2) stop seeing   ___a lemon

3) bully   ___get in shape

4) annoy   ___on someone's back

5) jog   ___pushy

■ **CLOZE IT**—Use one of the above expressions to complete the sentences. Be sure to check your grammar!

1) I broke down on the freeway because I drive _____!

2) My boss is_____about finishing the project before the deadline.

3) Irina is going to train for the marathon, so she needs to_____.

4) When Carlos moved overseas, he _____with his girlfriend.

5) He never listens to her! He only wants what he wants. He is so_____.

■ **SENSE OR NONSENSE**—With your classmates, discuss the sentences and decide if they do or don't make sense.

1) I love driving **a lemon** because I can really depend on it._____

2) It's better to be the person who **breaks up**._____

3) If you want to **get in shape**, eat more junk food._____

4) It's great when someone is **on your back**._____

5) **Pushy** people are easy to hang out with._____

■ **PLUG IT IN**—Use the expressions to replace the underlined words. Make sure to check your grammar! Check the Index/Glossary for words you may not know.

1) He's <u>always bugging me</u> about my weight. I know I'm fat. He should leave me alone.

2) Although she loved him, she had to <u>end the relationship</u> because he couldn't understand her.

3) Regina really bugs me with her <u>aggressive</u> attitude.

4) This car is <u>a piece of junk</u>. I'm getting rid of it.

5) Nelson is going to <u>train</u> for the triathlon, which is swimming, running, and cycling.

Questions to Ask Someone from Student Group 1

Ask Student 1 the following questions. He or she will tell you the answers. You should write down the answers. Student 1 can look at pages 72-73 to find the answers.

■ **TELL ME:** Ask Student 1 the following questions to get the expressions

1) How can you describe something that is useful?_____

2) What is a way to say someone talks too much?_____

3) What do you call a very good-looking man?_____

4) How can you say you feel comfortable with someone?_____

5) What is a way to say "I haven't seen you for awhile?"_____

■ **MAKE THIS MAKE SENSE:** Ask Student 1 to change these sentences to make sense.

1) **Hunks** don't usually make good models.

2) A good computer doesn't **come in handy** for doing homework.

3) I don't like to live with people I **get along with**.

4) I saw you five minutes ago. **Long time, no see**.

5) I really enjoy talking to Donna because she **talks my ears off**.

Questions to Ask Someone from Student Group 2

Ask Student 2 the following questions. He or she will tell you the answers. You should write down the answers. Student 2 can look at pages 74-75 to find the answers.

■ **TELL ME:** Ask Student 2 the following questions to get the expressions.

1) How can I ask if you remember something?_____

2) How can you describe someone who is very stable?_____

3) What is another way to say visit someone's house?_____

4) How are you described if you have a lot of energy at night?_____

5) Is there another way to say you can solve something?_____

■ **MAKE THIS MAKE SENSE:** Ask Student 2 to change these sentences to make sense.

1) You can **come over** to visit me after 3:00 a.m. No problem.

2) That **rings a bell.** I can't remember which way to go now.

3) It is really easy to **figure out** computer bugs.

4) **Morning people** usually go to bed very late.

5) Linda is working on her doctorate degree. She doesn't **have it together** at all.

Questions to Ask Someone from Student Group 3

Ask Student 3 the following questions. He or she will tell you the answers. You should write down the answers. Student 3 can look at pages 76-77 to find the answers.

■ **TELL ME:** Ask Student 3 following questions to get the expressions.

1) What is a word to describe a bad car?_____

2) How can you say you are ending a relationship?_____

3) If you train to get in good physical condition, you_____

4) Is there a word for someone who is very bossy?_____

5) What is a way to say someone is bothering you about something?_____

■ **MAKE THIS MAKE SENSE:** Ask Student 3 to change these sentences to make sense.

1) I'm going to **get in shape** by sitting in front of the TV and becoming a "couch potato".

2) **Breaking up** with someone you love is very easy to do.

3) **Pushy** people are so down-to-earth.

4) Most German and Japanese cars are **lemons**.

5) It's easy to be laid-back when someone is **on your back**.

Students 1—2—3

Before you begin the Halftime Activities, you must first complete pages 72-80 of Chapter 5. These activities are designed to get you to think about and discuss the meaning and use of the 15 expressions you have just studied.

■ **EXPRESSION GUIDE:** With your class, in small groups, or with friends, look over and talk about the idioms and slang you've been studying. Write down any extra information. Here are some questions to ask each other:

1) What kinds of people do you think use these expressions?
   (young, old, male, female...)

2) Where do you think you might hear these expressions?
   (school, beach, home, work, restaurant, nightclub, store...)

3) How do you think people say these expressions?
   (happy, angry, neutral, excited...)

EXPRESSION GUIDE

a hunk *slang*	talk someone's ears off	come in handy	get along	Long time no see.
ring a bell	come/go over	a morning/ night person	figure out	have/get it together *slang*
pushy	a lemon	break up	get in shape	on someone's back *slang*

■ **CIRCLE AND DISCUSS** key words or phrases that show the meaning of the expression. It's best to work with a partner.

1) I'm definitely **a night-person** because I can get most of my work done after 10:00 p.m. Sometimes I have to force myself to go to sleep!

2) Hey! **Long time no see**! How have you been doing? I can't even remember the last time we saw each other. Are you still with the same company?

3) I know it is her job, but that saleslady was way too **pushy**! She needs to learn to give customers some space so that they can think about what they want.

4) Ugh! I have such a headache. My colleague just **talked my ears off** about how much she can't stand our boss.

5) Come on! It's high time we **get in shape**! After everything we ate during the holidays, we've put on weight!

6) The Internet **comes in handy** for so many things! I use it to book my plane tickets, check out places to take my next vacation, buy concert tickets, find out about the latest movies, ...

7) Little Christopher is growing into quite the **hunk**! He's only 12 and he's already almost as tall as his dad. He doesn't realize how cute he is!

8) I believe what you are telling me, but I just don't remember doing that! It really **doesn't ring a bell**.

9) My neighbor's cat **doesn't get along** with my cat. They always try to beat each other up! They also hiss and meow at each other from the balconies.

10) Keiko has to **figure out** her new schedule: when she goes to school, when she works, when she has to study, and when she can have some fun!

11) My young neighbor, Brittany, loves to **come over** after school. She likes to look in my fridge and find something to eat and tell me about what she's doing in school.

12) Mei's folks are **on her back** about getting married. She doesn't want to think about it yet, but they think she should be someone's wife.

13) The first car I ever bought was **a real lemon**! It cost me more to fix it than it cost to buy it!

14) Jun is really **getting it together**. He's making long-term plans. He passed the TOEFL, and he has already met with an academic advisor. He's going to transfer from a community college to a university.

15) They **broke up**, but two months later they decided to get back together because they are really in love and they want to understand each other and communicate better.

■ **FIND OUT** about some grammar points and additional meanings of some expressions. Consult the Grammar Guide in Appendix E on page 181 for more information.

1) **break up**—The word **break** is highly idiomatic. Here are three more phrasal verbs using **break**. Match the definitions with the examples.

a) I ate too much chocolate and   **1) discovery**
      my skin **broke out.**___

b) My car **broke down** and I had to get   **2) got blemishes**
      it towed to the mechanic.___

c) Cancer researchers have been   **3) stop working**
      making **break-throughs.**___

2) on someone's back—The opposite of **on** is **off**. What do you think the following sentences mean?

    a) Would you **get off my back about** my hair? I like it this way!

    Meaning:_____

    b) My girlfriend is finally **off my back** about all my soccer games.

    Meaning:_____

3) get in shape—If the opposite of **in** is **out**, what do you think the sentences below mean?

    a) I was so tired after that hike in the mountains. I'm really **out of shape**.

    Meaning:_____

    b) Shin **is in great shape**! He eats well, sleeps a lot, and works out regularly.

    Meaning:_____

4) pushy—**Pushy** is an adjective, but you can also express the same meaning in the verb form. Fill in the blanks in the sentence below with the adjective or verb form.

    a) Don't be so_____with me. Stop trying to make me do things I don't want to do. If you continue to_____me, I'm out of here.

5) come in handy—**Handy** is also often used as an adjective. In this sense, **handy** and **neat** are sometimes synonyms. How would you describe the following?

    a) Look at the sunset! That's_____.

    b) This three-colored pen is really_____.

6) a hunk—There are many ways to describe men and women in English. Test your knowledge of this important topic!

    a) A good-looking young guy or girl is called a

        1) babe   **2)** chick   **3)** fox

    b) A guy who is strong, or thinks he is strong, and thinks women like him is called a

        1) fox   **2)** stud   **3)** horse

    c) Many young men, especially surfers, refer to young women as

        1) freaks   **2)** chicks   **3)** cats

■ **EXPRESSION LOG:** (1) Choose 10 expressions from this chapter to practice by writing original sentences, then (2) add two new expressions that you hear. Follow the New Expression Guide in Appendix A on page 159.

You are going to listen to 15 stories. Read the endings of the stories below before you begin. Be sure you understand the vocabulary. Then listen to the stories one by one to find the expression that completes the sentence.

1) _____ for two hours about how many mistakes they made!

2) _____ at first, but finally something was familiar.

3) _____ when he kept asking us to dance even though we had told him no.

4) _____ because I can use it whenever I need to.

5) _____ because she always has plans to improve herself.

6) _____! All the girls at school seem to like him.

7) _____ our place at 8:30.

8) _____. He says he feels great and has a lot of energy.

9) _____ well. If I need anything, I know I can ask them.

10) _____ how to input the phone numbers in my new telephone.

11) _____. I'm glad we could trade it in for a new one!

12) _____ about how messy he is all the time.

13) _____. You haven't changed at all!

14) _____. By the time everyone else gets up, she's ready to start her day.

15) _____ with him because there was no compromise.

RULES:
- Roll the die: If the number is three or less, choose an expression to use in a short story. (1 point)

  If the number more than three, choose two expressions to use in a short story. (2 points)
- You must finish telling your story within one minute.
- If you use another expression in your story, it is worth 1 more point.
- Each expression may be used only three times. Check them off as they are used.
- The first person to reach 21 wins.

come over 1___ 2___ 3___	pushy 1___ 2___ 3___	figure out 1___ 2___ 3___	long time no see 1___ 2___ 3___	have it together 1___ 2___ 3___
talk someone's ears off 1___ 2___ 3___	get in shape 1___ 2___ 3___	a lemon 1___ 2___ 3___	come in handy 1___ 2___ 3___	a morning person 1___ 2___ 3___
break up 1___ 2___ 3___	get along 1___ 2___ 3___	ring a bell 1___ 2___ 3___	a hunk 1___ 2___ 3___	be on some- one's back 1___ 2___ 3___

Keep Score

Name	Name	Name	Name

a lemon

6

have a crush on

a know-it-all

stress out

neat

easy come, easy go

shape up or ship out

be into

a steal

run into

fake

folks

show up

stuck-up

stick with

play the field

Student Group 1

Learn the meanings of the following five expressions by completing the exercises. Work with Student Group 1 or by yourself.

■ **GUESS** the meanings of the five expressions.

1) That guy really bugs me because he is such **a know-it-all**.

2) My job **stresses me out** because I have too much to do.

3) Your work sounds **neat**. You get to travel and make money!

4) When I was 12, I **had a crush on** my swimming coach. I couldn't wait for swim practice!

5) You win some and you lose some. **Easy come, easy go**.

■ **CHECK OUT** the definitions and examples of the expressions.

1) a know-it-all—a person who acts like they know everything even if they don't.
   Watch out. Here comes "Mr. Know-it-all". He'll tell you what to do even if you don't ask.

2) stress out—make or become very tired from pressure or tension.
   We argue so much with each other that I'm totally stressed out.

3) neat—cool, excellent, great, clean.
   What a neat mountain bike you have. It's so light too.

4) have a crush on—like someone, have special feelings for someone, puppy love
   Have you ever had a crush on your teacher?

5) Easy come, easy go—what you can easily get you can also easily lose; not take things seriously.
   When you go to Las Vegas, it's better to think easy come, easy go about money.

■ **QUICK FIX**—Match the expressions to the words that are similar.

1) tense   ___have a crush on

2) super   ___stressed out

3) whatever happens is ok ___ a know-it-all

4) presumptuous ___ neat

5) like ___ easy come, easy go

■ **CLOZE IT**—Use one of the expressions to complete the sentences. Be sure to check your grammar!

1) Ralph is a terrible boyfriend because of his_____attitude.

2) Ms. Jones acts like _____at work and tells everyone what to do.

3) That is a really_____painting. Where did you get it?

4) All work and no play makes me feel very_____.

5) I think Bruce_____ Daniela, the actress from Mexico. That is why he is learning Spanish.

■ **SENSE OR NONSENSE**—With your classmates, discuss the sentences and decide if they do or don't make sense.

1) When you feel **stressed out**, you should go for a massage._____

2) Sometimes it is good to have an **easy come, easy go** way of thinking._____

3) People who act like **know-it-alls** are never insecure with themselves._____

4) If you clean your room, it will be **neat**._____

5) Most people never **have crushes on** anyone._____

■ **PLUG IT IN**—Use the expressions to replace the underlined words. Make sure to check your grammar. Check the Index/Glossary for words you may not know.

1) Su-Jung is such a sweetheart that every guy <u>wants to get to know her</u>.

2) My new color printer is really <u>great</u>. The pictures come out so clear.

3) If your heart gets broken, remember <u>there are plenty of "fish in the sea"</u>.

4) Olivier is so annoying to hang out with because he <u>acts like the expert</u>.

5) When we feel <u>uptight</u> at work, we sometimes go out for a happy hour.

Student Group 2

Learn the meanings of the following five expressions by completing the exercises. Work with Student Group 2 or by yourself.

■ **GUESS** the meanings of the five expressions.

1) When I was a teenager, my parents told me to **shape up or ship out**.

2) Lisa **is into** skiing.

3) This was **a steal**! I only paid $40.00 *bucks*.

4) You'll never guess who I **ran into** at the store yesterday!

5) That is not real leather. It's **fake**.

■ **CHECK OUT** the definitions and examples of the expressions.

1) **shape up or ship out**—improve your behavior or leave.
   When Hiro didn't do his assignment again, the teacher told him to shape up or ship out.

2) **be into**—very interested in, have a hobby.
   Theyab is into French movies these days. He sees one twice a week.

3) **a steal**—buy something of high quality for a low price, very inexpensive.
   I can't believe you only paid $100.00 for that sofa. What a steal!

4) **run into**—see someone by accident, unplanned.
   We keep running into each other all over town! How funny.

5) **fake**— not real or authentic, superficial.
   Tracy only cares about the way she looks. She is so fake.

■ **QUICK FIX**—Match the expressions to the words that are similar.

1) cheap ___be into

2) not genuine ___run into

3) like to do a lot ___fake

4) better behave ___a steal

5) meet by chance ___shape up or ship out

■ **CLOZE IT**—Use one of the above expressions to complete the sentences. Be sure to check your grammar!

1) Glen_____ getting in shape. He goes to the gym almost every day.

2) We were so lucky to get this car. It was_____.

3) I_____ my old professor at the theater last night. He didn't remember my name, but he remembered my face.

4) I told my roommate to_____ otherwise I'd have to look for someone else to live with.

5) It may look like a diamond, but it is_____.

■ **SENSE OR NONSENSE**—With your classmates, discuss the sentences and decide if they do or don't make sense.

1) **Running into** someone you know can be funny._____

2) **Fake** people make good buddies._____

3) When a store has a great sale, some of the things are **a steal**._____

4) If your boss tells you to **shape up or ship out**, you had better listen._____

5) It's good to **be into** things that you enjoy._____

■ **PLUG IT IN**—Use the expressions to replace the underlined words. Make sure to check your grammar. Check the Index/Glossary for words you may not know.

1) Ben had better <u>change his attitude</u> at work or else he is going to lose his job.

2) I can't believe you bought that whole new stereo system for under $500.00. What <u>a bargain</u>.

3) These aren't Armani jeans. They're <u>a great imitation</u>.

4) I <u>saw</u> Gary at the supermarket. We hadn't seen each other for at least seven years!

5) Oscar <u>has become more and more interested in</u> computers these days.

Student Group 3

Learn the meanings of the following five expressions by completing the exercises. Work with Student Group 3 or by yourself.

■ **GUESS** the meanings of the five expressions.

1) I'm going to my **folks** for the holidays.

2) Everybody **showed up** late for the party.

3) Beatrice lives in her **stuck-up**, high-society world.

4) Diane has to **stick with** her diet otherwise she'll never lose weight.

5) Derrick likes to **play the field** and date lots of women.

■ **CHECK OUT** the definitions and examples of the expressions.

1) folks—parents, family members, people
   I usually go over to my folks for dinner once or twice a month.

2) show up—arrive, come
   What time do you think they'll show up?

3) stuck-up—snobby, conceited
   People who only want money are often also stuck-up.

4) stick with—not quit, don't give up
   English is hard to learn, but I'm going to stick with it.

5) play the field—go out with many different people
   You ought to play the field when you're young.

■ **QUICK FIX**—Match the expressions to the words that are similar..

1) vain   ___play the field

2) keep at it   ___folks

3) appear   ___stick with it

4) date   ___stuck-up

5) mom and dad   ___show up

■ **CLOZE IT**—Use one of the above expressions to complete the sentences. Be sure to check your grammar!

1) If we _____ five minutes late, we won't get in.

2) Ugh, I can't stand his _____ attitude, just because he drives a Porsche.

3) Your _____ seem like really nice people. I enjoyed meeting them.

4) I'm totally beat, but I _____ and finished the 10K run.

5) Watch out girls! Don Juan is in town, ready to _____.

■ **SENSE OR NONSENSE**—With your classmates, discuss the sentences and decide if they do or don't make sense.

1) **Stuck-up** people are really down-to-earth. _____

2) A loyal girlfriend will **play the field** while she is seeing you. _____

3) The **folks** I work with are really friendly, so we get along well. _____

4) She **stuck with it** and started smoking again. _____

5) In some cultures, it's normal to **show up** really late for a party. _____

■ **PLUG IT IN**—Use the expressions to replace the underlined words. Make sure to check your grammar. Check the Index/Glossary for words you may not know.

1) I have to <u>follow</u> my budget to save enough money to pay tuition for the next school term.

2) The <u>people</u> who work in the office are super helpful.

3) <u>Going out with lots of people</u> can be exciting for a while.

4) Rafael never <u>comes</u> to class on time because he's always in the computer lab.

5) Corina is one of the most <u>egotistical</u> people I have ever met. She thinks she is so great!

Questions to Ask Someone from Student Group 1

Ask Student 1 the following questions. He or she will tell you the answers. You should write down the answers. Student 1 can look at pages 88-89 to find the answers.

■ **TELL ME:** Ask Student 1 the following questions to get the expressions.

1) What is another word for great or wonderful? _neat_

2) Is there a word for someone who thinks they know everything? _a know it all_

3) What is a way to say you like someone? _a crush on_

4) If you are under a lot of pressure, how do you feel? _extressed out_

5) Is there an expression to describe easily winning or losing? _easy come easy go_

■ **MAKE THIS MAKE SENSE:** Ask Student 1 to change these sentences to make sense.

1) I care too much about money. **Easy come, easy go.**
   I don't care very

2) I **have a huge crush on** Michael because he is such a nerd.
   sweety

3) **Know-it-alls** are always right about whatever they say.
   are not it all

4) **Neat** people make bad roommates.
   good

5) Being **stressed out** is good for your health.
   Being stressed out it Bad out

Questions to Ask Someone from Student Group 2

Ask Student 2 the following questions. He or she will tell you the answers. You should write down the answers. Student 2 can look at pages 90-91 to find the answers.

■ **TELL ME:** Ask Student 2 the following questions to get the expressions.

1) How can I say that, by chance, I saw someone I know? _run in to_

2) Is there a way to say you'd better behave or leave? _Shape up oor ship out_

3) Is there another way to say something isn't real? _Fake_

4) What is another way to say you're interested in something? _be in to_

5) What can I call something that was really inexpensive? _steal_

■ **MAKE THIS MAKE SENSE:** Ask Student 2 to change these sentences to make sense.

1) It would not be surprising to **run into** an old classmate in an airport on the other side of the world. _it would be very_

2) You don't save any money if you purchase something that's **a steal**. _you save some money_

3) I wouldn't care if I bought a **fake** diamond for a lot of money! _would care_

4) If you**'re into** something, you usually feel bored. _run into_

5) Do whatever you want. **Shape up or ship out**. _you do whatever_

Questions to Ask Someone from Student Group 3

Ask Student 3 the following questions. He or she will tell you the answers. You should write down the answers. Student 3 can look at pages 92-93 to find the answers.

■ **TELL ME:** Ask Student 3 following questions to get the expressions.

1) Is there a way to say you go out with a lot of different people? _play the feeld_

2) How can I describe someone who thinks they are better than others? _stuck up_

3) What is another way to say arrive? _show up_

4) What is a friendly word for people? _folk_

5) Is there another expression that means don't give up? _stik with it_

■ **MAKE THIS MAKE SENSE:** Ask Student 3 to change these sentences to make sense.

1) Don't **stick with** your project if you want to finish it.

2) **Stuck-up** people never like to show off.

3) You should **play the field** after you get married.

4) Teachers never call students **folks**.

5) It's OK to **show up** late for the TOEFL test.

Students 1—2—3

Before you begin the Halftime Activities, you must first complete pages 88-96 of Chapter 6. These activities are designed to get you to think about and discuss the meaning and use of the 15 expressions you have just studied.

■ **EXPRESSION GUIDE:** With your class, in small groups, or with friends, look over and talk about the idioms and slang you've been studying. Write down any extra information. Here are some questions to ask each other:

1) What kinds of people do you think use these expressions?
   (young, old, male, female...)

2) Where do you think you might hear these expressions?
   (school, beach, home, work, restaurant, nightclub, store...)

3) How do you think people say these expressions?
   (happy, angry, neutral, excited...)

EXPRESSION GUIDE

a know-it-all	stress out	neat *slang*	have a crush on	easy come, easy go
shape up or ship out	be into	a steal *slang*	run into	fake
folks	show up	stuck-up	stick with	play the field

■ **CIRCLE AND DISCUSS** key words or phrases that show the meaning of the expression. It's best to work with a partner.

1) We can't give up now! We're not going to quit. It's hard, but we have to **stick with it**. No pain, no gain!

2) I have **a huge crush on** Kevin. He is a crack-up and he's quite a hunk! In fact, I'm nuts about him.

3) We **ran into** Michael at Bellagio Hotel Casino in Las Vegas! He moved there three years ago. What a coincidence!

4) I'm going to my **folks** for Thanksgiving. My mom is going to cook the turkey. I'll make the pie. My sister will do the potatoes and salad, and my brother will eat!

5) Laura has always been outspoken, but she is **a know-it-all** now. She was telling me how to do my job, but she has never worked in my field.

6) Jeremy was told to **shape up or ship out** if he didn't start to follow the rules like everyone else on his soccer team.

7) I'm really tired of her **easy come, easy go** attitude. She needs to learn to take responsibility for her actions. Someday her parents won't be there to help her.

8) A lot of people decorate their houses with artificial plants. They look real, but they're **fake**.

9) Abraham **is playing the field**. He goes out with about four different women at the same time. What a busy guy!

10) My computer was **a steal**! I think I saved over $300.00! I was able to take advantage of the sale because I have a friend who works at the computer store and I qualified for the first-time buyer discount!

11) The concert is supposed to start in 10 minutes, but look at all these empty seats! If people don't **show up**, I wonder if we can get closer to the stage.

12) I love your paintings. They're really **neat**. I like the colors, the texture, and the dreamlike quality. The frames are great too.

13) Lisa **is into** black and white photography. She takes the pictures, develops them, and then paints them. Her work is really cool.

14) Jean was so **stressed out** from work that she decided to call in sick to take the day off so she could just kick back, relax, and do as little as possible.

15) I didn't like that couple. They complained about everything at the restaurant. Nothing was good enough for them. I think they were really **stuck-up**.

■ **FIND OUT** about some grammar points and additional meanings of some expressions. Consult the Grammar Guide in Appendix E on page 181 for more information.

1) **stress out**—This expression can be a separable phrasal verb, **stress someone out**, or it can be a participle adjective, **be stressed out**. Complete the sentences below with an appropriate form of **stress out**.

   a) I can't stand working 50 hours a week. It_____.

   b) Pascal decided to take a long vacation because he_____.

2) **be into**—This expression is followed by a gerund phrase or noun phrase. Read the examples below and decide if the underlined expressions are gerunds or nouns. Then supply your own.

  a) When I was a teenager, I was into building model airplanes.

  gerund or noun? Your own:_____

  b) I've gotten into photography lately.

  gerund or noun? Your own:_____

3) **fake**—This expression has some interesting variations. It can be an adjective, a noun, or a verb. Read the sentences below and match them to their grammatical category and definition.

a) That girl seems really fake._____	**1)** noun	**1)** pretend
b) I had to fake it to get the job done.____	**2)** adjective	**2)** superficial
c) This Rolex watch is a fake._____	**3)** verb	**3)** not authentic

4) **run into**—We studied that this expression means to meet someone you already know by chance, but it can also literally mean to **run into**—crash or bump into someone or something. **Run** is highly idiomatic. Check out some more common expressions with run and see if you can match them to their definition.

a) I'm late! I've got to **run** now!___	**1)** crash
b) Oh no! You **ran into** a tree?___	**2)** finish using
c) He **ran out of** gas!___	**3)** hurry, leave

5) **play the field**—There are some other important expressions associated with **play**. It is fine to **play the field** and go out with a lot of people. But it is also important to be honest and not **play games**. Sometimes people who **play games** are called **players**. **Players** can also be business people who are willing to take risks. Complete the sentences below with the best expression of **play**.

  a) Mark told her he didn't have a girlfriend, but it's not true.
  He_____with her.

  b) Be careful ladies. That hunk is also_____!

6) **stick with it**—This expression has a sister expression: **stick it out**, which means the same as stick with it. There is another expression similar in form: **get stuck with**, which means to be left with the responsibility. What do you think the following sentence means?

  a) Why am I the one who **gets stuck with** doing all the dishes?
  Meaning:_____

■ **EXPRESSION LOG:** (1) Choose 10 expressions from this chapter to practice by writing original sentences, then (2) add two new expressions that you hear. Follow the New Expression Guide in Appendix A on page 159.

Listen to the situations. Write the expression you hear. Then answer the following: Was it a question____? or a statement____.
How was it said? Happy___ Neutral___ Irritated___

1. _____ _____ ___?___ . H__ N__ I__	2. _____ _____ ___?___ . H__ N__ I__	3. _____ _____ ___?___ . H__ N__ I__	4. _____ _____ ___?___ . H__ N__ I__	5. _____ _____ ___?___ . H__ N__ I__
6. _____ _____ ___?___ . H__ N__ I__	7. _____ _____ ___?___ . H__ N__ I__	8. _____ _____ ___?___ . H__ N__ I__	9. _____ _____ ___?___ . H__ N__ I__	10. _____ _____ ___?___ . H__ N__ I__
11. _____ _____ ___?___ . H__ N__ I__	12. _____ _____ ___?___ . H__ N__ I__	13. _____ _____ ___?___ . H__ N__ I__	14. _____ _____ ___?___ . H__ N__ I__	15. _____ _____ ___?___ . H__ N__ I__

RULES: Questions: YES/NO? INFORMATION? STATEMENT?
- Roll the die:
- If the number is below three, choose an expression and make a YES/NO question._____Y/N
- If the number is over three, choose an expression and make an INFOR-MATION question._____I
- If your number is THREE, make a STATEMENT question._____S
- Each expression can be used once for each category. Write your name in the box.
- You have 20 seconds to think of how to use your expression.
- Be sure to answer each other's questions.

stick with it	be into	a know-it-all	easy come, easy go	run into
_____Y/N	_____Y/N	_____Y/N	_____Y/N	_____Y/N
_____I	_____I	_____I	_____I	_____I
_____S	_____S	_____S	_____S	_____S
a steal	play the field	folks	stress out	have a crush on
_____Y/N	_____Y/N	_____Y/N	_____Y/N	_____Y/N
_____I	_____I	_____I	_____I	_____I
_____S	_____S	_____S	_____S	_____S
shape up or ship out	neat	stuck-up	fake	show up
_____Y/N	_____Y/N	_____Y/N	_____Y/N	_____Y/N
_____I	_____I	_____I	_____I	_____I
_____S	_____S	_____S	_____S	_____S

Password

RULES:
- Choose a partner to form a team of two: Player 1 and Player 2. There will be Team A and Team B.
- Each round is three minutes. The goal is to write as many expressions as possible.
  Spelling counts! If you misspell an expression, you lose it!

ROUND 1
- Team A Player 1 and Team B Player 1 turn to page 106.
- Team A Player 2 and Team B Player 2 listen to the clues and write the expression in the Password Grid #1.

ROUND 2
- Team A Player 2 and Team B Player 2 turn to page 107.
- Team A Player 1 and Team B Player 1 listen to the clues and write the expression in the Password Grid #2.

Password Round 1

1.	6.
2.	7.
3.	8.
4.	9.
5.	10.

SCORE: Team A____   Team B____

Password Round 2

1.	6.
2.	7.
3.	8.
4.	9.
5.	10.

SCORE: Team A____   Team B____

Dialogue Match

Partner A: Begin the dialogue. Read your first line to Partner B.
Partner B: Listen to Partner A and choose the best response.
NUMBER the exchanges!

Partner A	**Partner B**
___Oh, right. Friday *Bumper-to-bumper* traffic. Are you still working at the same place?	___Good for you! How are your **folks**?
___Hey, **Long time, no see**! How have you been doing?	___I'd love to. Your Dad has always been so **down-to-earth**.
___That's really **neat**. You've always been **open-minded** at work. Well, I've got to run now. Look forward to seeing you Friday!	___What a surprise! Wow, you look super! You've really **gotten in shape**. How have you been doing?
___Yeah, he **gets along** well with everyone. **Come over** around 7:00.	___I'm still with the same company. We **went through** a lot of management changes and now we finally **have it together**!
___Really well. I **got into** cycling last year and I've **been sticking to** a healthy diet lately. No *junk food* for me!	___I probably won't **show up** till after 8:00. I usually don't **make good time** in Friday traffic after work.
___They're fine. My Dad is going to retire soon. We're having a little **get-together** this Friday. Why don't you **come over**?	___So do I. I'm glad we **ran into** each other. See you Friday!

Password Round 1

Team A Player 1 and Team B Player 1. Below are 10 expressions which you must explain to your partner. He/she will write down the expression you are describing. You must not say the expression! You can describe them in any order you wish. Remember, you have three minutes to make your partner guess all ten expressions!

1) a backseat driver

2) pushy

3) see someone

4) have a crush on

5) fake

6) in hot water

7) break up

8) get over

9) stuck-up

10) be on someone's back

The Great Egghead Race

In teams of two, unscramble the expressions and write an original sentence. Whichever team finishes first is the Egghead Winner! Three out of five wins!

1) pehsapuoriphstou_____

    Sentence:_____

2) rasepoongimrn_____

    Sentence:_____

3) eocmnnihyad_____

    Sentence:_____

4) tlesaa_____

    Sentence:_____

5) ypalamegs_____

    Sentence:_____

Password Round 2

Team A Player 2 and Team B Player 2. Below are 10 expressions which you must explain to your partner. He/she will write down the expression you are describing. You must not say the expression! You can describe them in any order you wish. Remember, you have three minutes to make your partner guess all ten expressions!

1) hunk

2) in the same boat

3) a lemon

4) a know-it-all

5) easy come, easy go

6) figure out

7) a sweet tooth

8) blind date

9) play the field

10) ring a bell

Grand Finale

Work with one or two partners to write a dialogue or a story using a minimum of 20 expressions from Chapters 4-5-6 and from your Expression Logs. There is no maximum, so use as many expressions as possible! Your teacher may announce winners!

stuck-up

7

keep an eye on

a knockout

come up with

hot

hit the sack

a chicken

take turns

nosy

drop off

back in a flash

work out

step on it

loaded

a brain

put one's foot in one's mouth

PART I Work It Out

Student Group 1

Learn the meanings of five expressions by completing the following exercises.
Work with Student Group 1 or by yourself.

■ **GUESS** the meanings of the five expressions.

1) Most people think Cindy Crawford is a **knockout**. *for man atracsion hunk*

2) We **came up with** the best idea for our final project! *en contru la solucion. finde solution.*

3) Antonio Banderas is definitely **hot** right now. You can see his face everywhere. *popiulas sexsy popular*

4) I'm going to **hit the sack** because I'm so beat. *dormir go to slep =bet to day berty taller*

5) Would you **keep an eye on** my suitcase while I run to the restroom? *(watch) echarle un vistaso. a me cos poo dos dias voy asalir the vacaciones*

■ **CHECK OUT** the definitions and examples of the expressions.

1) **a knockout**—a very attractive person, usually a woman.
   When you're dressed to kill, you look like a knockout.

2) **come up with**—think of an idea or solution, figure out.
   Nicholas came up with a solution to fix the bug in the software.

3) **hot**—extremely popular or successful.
   The hot look for young guys nowadays is getting one ear pierced.

4) **hit the sack**—go to sleep
   It's already midnight. Time to hit the sack. I've got to get up early tomorrow.

5) **keep an eye on**—watch, look after
   The teacher kept an eye on Tony because he usually tries to cheat.

■ **QUICK FIX**—Match the expressions to the words that are similar.

1) go to bed   _2_ keep an eye on *cuidar*

2) guard   _5_ a knockout *mujer atiativa*

3) create   _1_ hit the sack *voy a dormir*

4 trendy: *3 some up with*

5 gorgeous   *4 hot*

4) trendy   *3* come up with

5) gorgeous   *4* hot

■ **CLOZE IT**—Use one of the above expressions to complete the sentences. Be sure to check your grammar!

1) I only slept four hours last night, so tonight I'm going to *hit the sack* early.

2) Would you *keep an eye on* my house while I'm on vacation?

3) That guy was a total hunk. What *a knockout* !

4) We still have to *come up with* a time to have our next meeting.

5) Knee-high black boots are the *hot* fashion trend this winter.

■ **SENSE OR NONSENSE**—With your classmates, discuss the sentences and decide if they do or don't make sense.

1) Sofia Loren has been **a knockout** her whole life. *S*

2) Most people don't like to buy whatever is **hot**. *NS*

3) I hate to **hit the sack** when I'm tired. *NS*

4) Benjamin Franklin didn't **come up with** many ideas during his life. *NS*

5) Larry asked me to **keep an eye on** his dog, so I don't have to feed it. *NS*

■ **PLUG IT IN**—Use the expressions to replace the underlined words. Make sure to check your grammar! Check the Index/Glossary for words you may not know.

1) Hawaii is still a very *hot* popular place for honeymooners.

2) Valeria is *one of the biggest* one of the most *a knockouts* stunning women I've ever seen.

3) I can't seem to *come up with* think of a good way to finish my paper.

4) I *keep an eye on my neighbor house* watered the plants and brought in the mail for my neighbor.

5) I went to bed at 3:00 a.m. What a night person I am.
I hit the sack

Student Group 2

Learn the meanings of the following five expressions by completing the exercises. Work with Student Group 2 or by yourself.

■ **GUESS** the meanings of the five expressions.

1) Don't be a chicken. Come on—give it a shot! *~tryed~ intentalo*
   no tengas miedo / no tegas mied

2) It's really important to take turns in class so that everyone can speak.
   toma tu turno

3) My neighbors are so nosy! They're always asking me what I'm doing.
   metiche

4) Would you drop me off at the store on your way home?
   destino. can you drop me off a my house tonight
   can you take a my house / mandar / repartir

5) Hang on! I'll be back in a flash. *give a right*
   regresar rapido / came back quickly

■ **CHECK OUT** the definitions and examples of the expressions.

1) a chicken—someone who is afraid to do or try something.
   I wanted to go parachuting, but I'm a big chicken!

2) take turns—one person does something after another person, not at the same time.
   We took turns singing karaoke at the party. It was a blast!

3) nosy—overly interested in other people's business.
   It's normal for mothers to be nosy about what their kids are doing.

4) drop off—take someone or something to a certain destination.
   I have to drop this off at the post office before work.

5) back in a flash—return quickly.
   I'm going to rent a video. I'll be back in a flash.

■ **QUICK FIX**—Match the expressions to the words that are similar.

1) deliver   2 nosy

2) too curious   5 take turns

3) come back quickly 1 drop off

4) scared   3 back in a flash

5) share   4 a chicken   *a brave a fraid*
   sherr   *to scared*

■ **CLOZE IT**—Use one of the above expressions to complete the sentences. Be sure to check your grammar!

1) Sometimes I think my roommate is _nosy_ because she asks me so many questions.

2) We're out of milk. I'll run to the store. _back in a flash_!

3) It's only fair to _take turns_ with all the work we have to do.

4) Ken didn't ask anyone to dance because he's _a chiken_.

5) Seth wants to _drop off_ his stuff because he doesn't want to bring it.

■ **SENSE OR NONSENSE**—With your classmates, discuss the sentences and decide if they do or don't make sense.

1) I'll be **back in a flash**—in about two hours. _NS_

2) It's easy to trust **nosy** people. _NS_ trust

3) **Chickens** usually love extreme sports. _NS_

4) People usually **drop off** their videos when they return them. _S_

5) Polite people never **take turns**. _NS_

■ **PLUG IT IN**—Use the expressions to replace the underlined words. Make sure to check your grammar!   Check the Index/Glossary for words you may not know.

1) Bruce asks too many questions about my personal life.
   nosy

2) My husband and I share the responsibility of driving our children to school.
   take turn

3) We were cowards when it was our turn to jump.
   shiken

4) I'll be here before you know it!
   I be back in flash.

5) I'll take this to the bank and then I'll be home.
   drop off

Student Group 3

Learn the meanings of the following five expressions by completing the exercises. Work with Student Group 3 or by yourself.

■ **GUESS** the meanings of the five expressions.

1) Doug works out at the gym four days a week.
gimnasio

2) Step on it! We're late!!!
pisar me el aselerador

3) Cristina Onassis was loaded.
cargado

4) Stephen Hawking has figured out a lot about the universe. What a brain.

5) He put his foot in his mouth when he asked about her age.

■ **CHECK OUT** the definitions and examples of the expressions.

1) work out—to exercise, to figure out, solve.
   We worked out the problem with the mail delivery. Now everyone is getting their mail like they should.

2) step on it—go faster, usually drive faster.
   Hey—don't drive so slowly! Step on it!

3) loaded—be very wealthy, have lots of equipment or accessories.
   This car has everything. It's fully loaded.

4) a brain—very intelligent.   *intelijente*
   She is such a brain that she skipped from 5th grade to 7th grade.

5) put one's foot in one's mouth—say something embarrassing or inappropriate.
   I shouldn't have asked about their divorce. I think I put my foot in my mouth.

■ **QUICK FIX**—Match the expressions to the words that are similar.

1) fully equipped   4 put your foot in your mouth *desir al iquiboceado*

2) super smart   5 work out

3) speed up   2 a brain *intelligente*

4) say something wrong   1 loaded *cargado*

5) do aerobics   3 step on it *pisar* *step on it*

112   Join the Club—Level 1

■ **CLOZE IT**—Use one of the expressions to complete the sentences. Be sure to check your grammar!

1) We need to make good time, so _step on it_.

2) My computer system is completely _loaded_. It's state-of-the-art.

3) He's _foot on his mouth = desir algo equivocado_ again. When will he learn to watch what he says?

4) Einstein was one of the biggest _brain_ that ever lived.

5) I like to _work out_ with my friend. We lift weights together.

■ **SENSE OR NONSENSE**—With your classmates, discuss the sentences and decide if they do or don't make sense.

1) I had to take the same class over three times because I'm such **a brain**. _NS_

2) You should **work out** if you want to get in shape. _S_

3) You don't have to pay extra if you want your car to be fully **loaded**. _NS_

4) **Step on it** so we can arrive at the party late. _NS_

5) If you **put your foot in your mouth**, people sometimes don't say anything. _S_

■ **PLUG IT IN**—Use the expressions to replace the underlined words. Make sure to check your grammar! Check the Index/Glossary for words you may not know.

1) I can't believe I said that. I feel really embarrassed.
put your foot in your mounth

2) Let's see how fast this Porsche goes. I'm going to punch it! _porsche step on it_
step on it

3) Peter figured out a good solution to the problem with the schedule.
work out

4) Leo is extremely bright. He can learn anything.
a brain

5) Howard Hughes was a billionnaire, but he was very ill so he couldn't enjoy his money.
loaded

PART II Information Gap

Questions to Ask Someone from Student Group 1

Ask Student 1 the following questions. He or she will tell you the answers. You should write down the answers. Student 1 can look at pages 108-109 to find the answers.

■ **TELL ME:** Ask Student 1 the following questions to get the expressions.

1) What is a way to say you want to think of some idea? *come up with*

2) How can I ask someone to watch something for me? *keep an eye on*

3) What can I call a very beautiful woman? *a knockout*

4) How can I say I'm going to bed? *hit the sack*

5) Is there a way to say something is super popular? *hot*

■ **MAKE THIS MAKE SENSE:** Ask Student 1 to change these sentences to make sense.

1) I have so much energy I want to **hit the sack**.
   go to bed

2) You don't have to **keep an eye on** my car if I leave the keys in it.
   guard

3) If someone is **hot**, no one wants to know about their life.
   trendy

4) Great teachers never **come up with** anything interesting to teach.
   create

5) Most fashion magazine cover models are not **knockouts**.
   gorgeous

Questions to Ask Someone from Student Group 2

Ask Student 2 the following questions. He or she will tell you the answers. You should write down the answers. Student 2 can look at pages 110-111 to find the answers.

■ **TELL ME:** Ask Student 2 the following questions to get the expressions.

1) Is there an expression meaning to bring someone somewhere? _drop off_

2) How can I tell someone that I'll be back really quickly? _back in flash_

3) What is an expression meaning to share fairly? _take turns_

4) What do I call someone who asks too many personal questions? _nosy_

5) What do you call someone who isn't brave? _a chicken_

■ **MAKE THIS MAKE SENSE:** Ask Student 2 to change these sentences to make sense.

1) He said, **"Back in a flash"** because it would take him a long time.
   comeback · buigle

2) A **nosy** person makes a good blind date.
   to corious

3) **Dropping off** a video in a drive-through is inconvenient.
   deliver

4) **A chicken** wouldn't be afraid to go backpacking in the Amazon rain forest.
   scured

5) It's not important to **take turns** when you have a conversation.
   shexr

Questions to Ask Someone from Student Group 3

Ask Student 3 the following questions. He or she will tell you the answers.
You should write down the answers. Student 3 can look at pages 112-113 to
find the answers.

■ **TELL ME:** Ask Student 3 following questions to get the expressions.

1) What can I call someone who is super smart? _a brain_

2) Is there a way to say someone is very rich? _loaded, loder_

3) How can I say I said something wrong that bugs someone? _put my foot in my mouth_

4) How can I tell someone to drive faster? _step on it_

5) What is another way to say that you exercise? _work out_

■ **MAKE THIS MAKE SENSE:** Ask Student 3 to change these sentences
to make sense.

1) We have plenty of time to get there, so **step on it**.
    speed up

2) People who **work out** usually spend most of their time in front of the TV.
    do erobics

3) People who are **loaded** can't buy anything they want.
    full equipped

4) Isaac Newton, who discovered gravity, was not **a brain**.
    super smart

5) I can make lots of friends if I often **put my foot in my mouth**.
    say something worong

Students 1—2—3

Before you start the Halftime Activities, you must first complete pages 108-116 of Chapter 7. These activities are designed to get you to think about and discuss the meaning and use of the 15 expressions you have just studied.

■ **EXPRESSION GUIDE:** With your class, in small groups, or with friends, look over and talk about the idioms and slang you've been studying. Write down any extra information. Here are some questions to ask each other:

1) What kinds of people do you think use these expressions?
   (*young, old, male, female...*)

2) Where do you think you might hear these expressions?
   (*school, beach, home, work, restaurant, nightclub, store...*)

3) How do you think people say these expressions?
   (*happy, angry, neutral, excited...*)

EXPRESSION GUIDE

a knockout	come up with	hot *slang*	hit the sack	keep an eye on
a chicken *slang*	take turns	nosy	drop off	back in a flash
work out	step on it	loaded *slang*	a brain	put one's foot in one's mouth

■ **CIRCLE AND DISCUSS** key words or phrases that show the meaning of the expression. It's best to work with a partner.

1) I've got to run to the post office and the bank. It'll take me about 20 minutes maximum. I'll be **back in a flash**.

2) That's a great idea! How did you **come up with** that? I would have never thought to do it that way. You're really creative!

3) I feel really good these days. I have lots of energy because I've been **working out**. I've been jogging in the mornings and doing yoga in the evenings.

4) We had a fun get-together last night. I got home late, but I still made it to my morning class. I'm really beat today, so I'll **hit the sack** early tonight.

5) I'm really curious and I don't mean to be **nosy**, but do you mind if I ask you how much money you make?

6) First he told her that she looked great. Then he told her she should work out more to get in better shape. He **put his foot in his mouth** again.

7) Are you going to be here for awhile? Great. Would you **keep an eye on** my books while I run to the cafeteria to grab a bite? I don't want to carry them with me.

8) After I fell out of the raft, I became **a chicken**. I'm afraid to go white water rafting again, especially on class 5 rapids.

9) Why do I always get behind a Sunday driver when I'm already late? I've got to pass this slowpoke and **step on it** pronto!

10) Kim had a little money to burn, so she bought herself a gorgeous Italian suit, an Ungaro. Look at her! What **a knockout**!

11) I **dropped Yoko off** at the mechanic again so that she could pick up her car, which unfortunately is a lemon. Poor Yoko!

12) When I was a kid, my sister and I had to **take turns** doing the chores, like washing the dishes and vacuuming. If we both shared our chores fairly, our folks gave us an allowance of $5.00 a week.

13) Anna is really **a brain**. She's only 12 years old, but she is such an outstanding student. She'll definitely get a scholarship for her college education.

14) Soccer is definitely the **hottest** sport in the world even though baseball and football are much more popular in the United States.

15) Michael Jordan makes about $300,000 every time he plays basketball, but he would have to save his entire income for 270 years to be as **loaded** as Bill Gates.

■ **FIND OUT** about some grammar points and additional meanings of some expressions. Consult the Grammar Guide in Appendix E on page 181 for more information.

1) hot—The slang expression **hot** has a few other common meanings. Look at the examples and match them to the best meaning.
   a) Wow, I'm **hot** tonight. Let's keep playing!___   **1)** stolen
   b) This jewelry is too cheap. It must be **hot**.___   **2)** spicy

c) Tall, dark and handsome. He's **hot.**___   **3)** winning

d) Indian food is very hot.___   **4)** sexy

2) ~~loaded~~—**Loaded** is another slang expression that has some other common meanings. We studied that **loaded** can mean to be very rich or to have all the extra equipment.   Guess three more meanings from the examples below.

a) What! He drank a six-pack of beer! He must be **loaded**!

b) It's an exciting day at the ballpark. The bases are **loaded**, and Mark McGuire is up to bat.

c) Don't ever play with a gun, **loaded** or not.

Meanings: *a)*_____   *b)*_____   *c)*_____

3) a brain—This expression can also be an adjective: **brainy**. Complete the sentence below with the grammatically correct form of **brain**.

a) Albert Einstein didn't seem very_____when he was a child because he didn't speak until he was five years old. However, he was one of the biggest_____that ever lived.

*Extra information: Guess the meaning below:

b) She is **the brains** in the family, not her husband._____

4) a chicken—The verb form of this expression is **chicken out**. It's a regular verb, and it has the same meaning as the noun counterpart: **a chicken**. Finish the sentence with the best form of **chicken**.

a) We_____of going camping last winter because it was just too cold for_____like us.

5) a knockout—This is another expression which has a verb form: **knock out**. It is a separable phrasal verb, and it is commonly associated with the sport of boxing. Supply the verb form of **knock out** in the sentences below:

a) Oscar de la Joya beat Julio Cesar Chavez because he_____.

b) Mike Tyson usually_____his opponents.

6) work out—This phrasal verb can be transitive or intransitive. If it means to exercise, it is intransitive—no object. If it means to solve or figure something out, it is transitive and separable. Remember, only transitive phrasal verbs can be separable. A related noun is **workout**, an exercise session. Identify the meaning and function of **work out** in the examples below:

a) We talked about the problem and then we **worked it out**.

_____

b) Todd **has been working out** almost every day.

_____

c) I had **a great workout** today. I feel really energetic.

_____

■ **EXPRESSION LOG:** (1) Choose 10 expressions from this chapter to practice by writing original sentences, then (2) add two new expressions that you hear. Follow the New Expression Guide in Appendix A on page 159.

Grammar Attack: Listen to each situation. Write the expression you hear.
Then answer the following:

• Was it said in the present, past or future?   ___pre ___pst ___fut
• Was it a question or a statement?   ___?   ___.

1. _____	2. _____	3. _____	4. _____	5. _____
_____	_____	_____	_____	_____
___pre ___pst ___fut	___pre ___pst ___fut	___pre ___pst ___fut	___pre ___pst ___fut	___pre ___pst ___fut
___? ___.	___? ___.	___? ___.	___? ___.	___? ___.
6. _____	7. _____	8. _____	9. _____	10. _____
_____	_____	_____	_____	_____
___pre ___pst ___fut	___pre ___pst ___fut	___pre ___pst ___fut	___pre ___pst ___fut	___pre ___pst ___fut
___? ___.	___? ___.	___? ___.	___? ___.	___? ___.
11. _____	12. _____	13. _____	14. _____	15. _____
_____	_____	_____	_____	_____
___pre ___pst ___fut	___pre ___pst ___fut	___pre ___pst ___fut	___pre ___pst ___fut	___pre ___pst ___fut
___? ___.	___? ___.	___? ___.	___? ___.	___? ___.

RULES: Roll the die and move ahead to the corresponding box. Use the expression as indicated. Total up the points you earn. The first person to reach 21 wins. Speak clearly! Grammar counts!

20. a brain	21. skip a turn	22. back in a flash	23. WILD DRAW	24. put one's foot in one's mouth
question, past 2 points	☹	future 1 point	☺ your choice affirmative, true 5 points	statement, true 3 points
19. work out	18. FREE CHOICE	17. miss a turn	16. take turns	15. come up with
simple present question 2 points	☺ 2 points	☹	negative 2 points	affirmative, past 3 points
10. hit the sack	11. WILD DRAW	12. nosy	13. lose a turn	14. step on it
information question 2 points	☺ your choice, negative, fact 5 points	past 2 points	☹	command 1 point
9. lose a turn	8. keep an eye on	7. a chicken	6. hot	5. FREE CHOICE
☹	polite request 4 points	statement 2 points	affirmative, false 3 points	☺ 1 point
START	1. a knockout	2. loaded	3. skip a turn	4. drop off
	simple question 2 points	present perfect 3 points	☹	future, offer 3 points

Keep Score

Name	Name	Name	Name

nosy

8

call it a day/night

turn down

lend a hand

wild

a shortcut

have time to kill

a bummer

luck out

get even

fish for compliments

sixth sense

get it

climb the walls

straighten up

tough

Student Group 1

Learn the meanings of the following five expressions by completing the exercises. Work with Student Group 1 or by yourself.

■ **GUESS** the meanings of the five expressions.

1) Sang-Hoon turned down the job offer because it wasn't what he really wanted.
   Say no = decir no

2) OK, we have worked enough on this. Let's call it a day.
   called it a day finish = terminado

3) Could you lend me a hand moving this weekend?
   lend me a hand : ayudar

4) The movie we saw last night was wild! You've got to check it out!!
   salvaje incontrolado violento, furioso

5) I discovered a shortcut to get to school . I saved five minutes.
   quick away : get away = tienes el camino rapido

■ **CHECK OUT** the definitions and examples of the expressions.

1) turn down—to reject or refuse.
   Shigeko turned down David's marriage proposal because he wanted to move to another country.

2) call it a day/night—end an activity, stop what you are doing.
   This party has been really fun, but I'm beat. Let's call it a night.

3) lend a hand—help, contribute, pitch in.
   That looks heavy. Let me lend you a hand.

4) wild—very exciting or crazy in a positive way.
   The football game was so close yesterday that the fans went wild!

5) a shortcut—a quicker way to get somewhere or do something.
   You don't have to take that road. Don't you know the shortcut?

■ **QUICK FIX**—Match the expressions to the words that are similar.

1) faster way   4 call it a day/night *terminado que esta asiendo*

2) stimulating   5 lend a hand *deme ayuda. obrindame una mano*

3) say no   a shortcut *comino corto*

4) finish   2 wild *wayld - salvaja - biolento*

5) give help   3 turn down *decir que no*

■ **CLOZE IT**—Use one of the above expressions to complete the sentences. Be sure to check your grammar!

1) We had a __wild__ time playing beach volleyball! Let's do that again soon!

2) I wanted to buy it, but I didn't need it, so I __turn down__ their offer. *oferta*

3) I know __shortcut__ to finish this assignment faster.
   do sometimeing faster: acer algo rapido

4) We've been working on this since 7:30 a.m. It's now 7:30 p.m. __let call it a day__

5) Ms. Farnes wants to move the chairs around. Let's __lend a hand__

■ **SENSE OR NONSENSE**—With your classmates, discuss the sentences and decide if they do or don't make sense.

1) We started 15 minutes ago. It's time to **call it a day**. __NS__

2) I didn't accept his offer, so I **turned him down**. __S__

3) Let's go to "Carnaval" in Brazil. It's supposed to be really **wild**! __S__

4) We made bad time because everyone **lent a hand**. __NS__

5) We made great time because of the **shortcut**. __S__

■ **PLUG IT IN**—Use the expressions to replace the underlined words. Make sure to check your grammar! Check the Index/Glossary for words you may not know.

1) All the neighbors <u>pitched in</u>, so we got all the moving done.
   lend a hand

2) This alley is a great <u>time-saver</u>, especially when there is so much traffic.
   shortcut

3) We've got to <u>hit the sack</u> now. It has been a really nice evening.
   Call it night

4) Our camping trip in the Rocky Mountains last summer was <u>so much fun</u>!
   wild

5) They made me a tempting offer with more money, but I had to <u>say no</u>.
   turn down

Student Group 2

Learn the meanings of the following five expressions by completing the exercises. Work with Student Group 2 or by yourself.

■ **GUESS** the meanings of the five expressions.

1) Linda isn't working right now, so she has some time to kill.
[handwritten: extra time. tiempo extra]

2) What a bummer about your car accident!
[handwritten: disappointed. no pasa el examen, disilusionar]

3) Wow, you really lucked out with your new job! That's fantastic.
[handwritten: good moment. buen momento / good job]

4) Be careful. He doesn't get mad. He gets even.
[handwritten: take revenge: I get's even with you]

5) Sally's fishing for compliments again about her new clothes.
[handwritten: tener buena noticias? o bien reporte ° O nadar muy bien en el spetaculo. O ser un buen nadador]

■ **CHECK OUT** the definitions and examples of the expressions.

1) **have time to kill**—have extra time, usually spent doing nothing important.
When I have time to kill, I like to people-watch.

2) **a bummer**—a disappointment.
This party is a bummer. Let's hit the road.

3) **luck out**—have a moment of very good luck.
Chris lucked out in Las Vegas last weekend and won $5,000.00.

4) **get even**—take revenge (not always in a negative way).
What? You were kidding! I'll get even with you for that!

5) **fish for compliments**—try to make someone say something nice about you.
Narrin was always fishing for compliments with his acting portfolio.

■ **QUICK FIX**—Match the expressions to the words that are similar.

1) very fortunate   *2* a bummer

2) too bad   *5* fish for compliments

3) get back at someone   *1* luck out

4) freetime   *3* get even

5) make someone notice something good   *4* have time to kill

■ **CLOZE IT**—Use one of the above expressions to complete the sentences. Be sure to check your grammar!

1) Bob cheated on his girlfriend, so she decided to _get even_.

2) Pam's new boyfriend is a hunk, is loaded, and he has a sweet tooth! She _lucked out_!

3) Our meeting got cancelled, so we _have time to kill_.

4) You can't go skiing with us? That's _a bummer_.

5) I'm not _fish for compliment_. I just want to know if you like my idea.

■ **SENSE OR NONSENSE**—With your classmates, discuss the sentences and decide if they do or don't make sense.

1) We **lucked out** and won a new car. _NS_

2) Members of organized crime families are famous for **getting even**. _S_

3) I'm so swamped that I **have time to kill**. _NS_

   ocupado
   I'm so. swamed o very busy

4) Some people **fish for compliments** because they're insecure. _S_

5) What **a bummer** that wonderful woman loves you. _NS_

■ **PLUG IT IN**—Use the expressions to replace the underlined words. Make sure to check your grammar! Check the Index/Glossary for words you may not know.

→spend time gastar tiempo

1) I <u>was hanging around</u> today, so I looked at old pictures.
   have time to kill

2) That is <u>a pity</u> he can't find a job nearby. _pity = pena lastima_
   a bummer

3) He's always <u>asking what I think of his work</u> and I always tell him it's great because it is. _fishing for compliment_

4) You <u>must feel thrilled</u>! You won the lottery!
   lucked out

5) He won't <u>hold that against you</u>. Don't worry. He'll forget about it <u>sooner or later</u>. _get even with you_

Student Group 3

Learn the meanings of the following five expressions by completing the exercises. Work with Student Group 3 or by yourself.

■ **GUESS** the meanings of the five expressions.

1) I'm not sure why, but my sixth sense tells me we should go.

2) Now he's going to get it. He put his foot in his mouth for the last time.

3) The weather was so horrible last winter that we were climbing the walls!

4) I'd like to straighten up my house before they come over.

5) Mr. James is a tough boss, but I respect him a lot.

■ **CHECK OUT** the definitions and examples of the expressions.

1) sixth sense—intuition (see, hear, taste, feel, smell).
   I have a feeling you will get the job. It's my sixth sense talking.

2) get it—be punished.
   You're going to get it if the teacher catches you cheating on the test.

3) climb the walls—feel extremely bored or stressed out.
   We're all climbing the walls at work because we're way too busy.

4) straighten up—make neat, clean.
   He needs to straighten up his desk. He can't find anything!

5) tough—difficult, hard.
   This test was really tough. I should have studied more.

■ **QUICK FIX**—Match the expressions to the words that are similar.

1) frustrated   _4_ tough

2) tidy   _3_ sixth sense

3) a hunch   _1_ climb the walls

4) challenging   _5_ get it

5) in hot water   _2_ straighten up

talley
consado

■ **CLOZE IT**—Use one of the above expressions to complete the sentences. Be sure to check your grammar.

1) Learning idioms is _____*tough*_____, but it's so useful.

2) I'm _____*straighten up*_____ because my neighbor's dog barks all night long!

3) Ugh! My closet is a mess. It's time to _____*clamb the walls*_____.

4) What? You crashed your folk's car because you were drinking! You're going to _____*get it*_____!

5) You had better listen to her because her _____*sixth sence*_____ is usually right.

■ **SENSE OR NONSENSE**—With your classmates, discuss the sentences and decide if they do or don't make sense.

1) If you speed, you might **get it** from the police. *S*

2) You can't explain your **sixth sense**. *S*

3) A good *amigo* **buddy** is **tough** to get along with. *ns*

4) It's easy to find things if you **straighten up** regularly. *ns*

5) **Climbing the walls** is a good way to kick back. *sn*

■ **PLUG IT IN**—Use the expressions to replace the underlined words. Make sure to check your grammar! Check the Index/Glossary for words you may not know.

1) Marie always feels calmer after she <u>cleans</u> her house.

2) Working out our problems is very <u>difficult</u>, but we can do it. *straighten up*

3) I'm <u>going nuts</u> with this stupid printer that keeps breaking down. What a lemon! *tough the wall* *climb the wall*

4) Paul is going to <u>be in trouble</u> when Joan finds out how much money he lost at the races. *ge it*

5) My <u>gut feeling</u> tells me that he won't come to the meeting. *sisth sense*

PART II Information Gap

Questions to Ask Someone from Student Group 1

Ask Student 1 the following questions. He or she will tell you the answers. You should write down the answers. Student 1 can look at pages 124-125 to find the answers.

■ **TELL ME:** Ask Student 1 the following questions to get the expressions.

1) What is way to say that something is very interesting and exciting? _wild_

2) Is there an idiom which means to reject? _Turned down_

3) What do you call a quicker way? _short cut_

4) What is a way to say you think you should finish? _lets call it a day_

5) How can I ask someone to help me? _lend a hend dend_

■ **MAKE THIS MAKE SENSE:** Ask Student 1 to change these sentences to make sense.

Madona a hasn made videos greasy

1) Madonna hasn't made very **wild** music videos.

You chould lend a hend

2) If you want to help someone, you shouldn't **lend a hand**.

you shodd kick back its help

3) After you **call it a day**, you shouldn't kick back.

Don't make you late

4) **Shortcuts** make you late.

Ficsther way turn down a bad a bad offer

5) Don't **turn down** a bad offer.

say no

Questions to Ask Someone from Student Group 2

Ask Student 2 the following questions. He or she will tell you the answers. You should write down the answers. Student 2 can look at pages 126-127 to find the answers.

■ **TELL ME:** Ask Student 2 the following questions to get the expressions.

1) Is there another way to say too bad? _a bummer_

2) What is a way to say you have extra time? _have time to kill_

3) How can you say you were very fortunate to get something? _luck out_

4) What is a way to make someone say something nice about you? _fish for compliment_

5) Is there another way to say revenge? _desquitarse_ _get even_

■ **MAKE THIS MAKE SENSE:** Ask Student 2 to change these sentences to make sense.

1) If someone is off _she's in_ your back, that can be **a bummer.**   _to bad_

2) Closed-minded people usually **luck out** a lot.   _very friendly_

3) If you're classy, you probably **fish for compliments.** _I'm a great_   _make some notice something good_

4) I have to get with it when I **have time to kill,**   _st_

5) If you like to **get even,** you have an easy come, easy go attitude.   _you don_   _you don't have to_   _get back at someone_

Questions to Ask Someone from Student Group 3

Ask Student 3 the following questions. He or she will tell you the answers. You should write down the answers. Student 3 can look at pages 128-129 to find the answers.

■ **TELL ME:** Ask Student 3 following questions to get the expressions.

1) Is there an expression which means very bored? _climb the wall_

2) What is another way to say to be in trouble? _get it_

3) Is there another word for intuition? _sixth sence_

4) How can I say to make something clean and neat? _straigten up_

5) What is another word to describe something difficult? _though_
   challenging

■ **MAKE THIS MAKE SENSE:** Ask Student 3 to change these sentences to make sense.

1) Handy things are **tough** to use.
   challenging

2) You are going to **get it** if you do the right thing.
   in hot water

3) You shouldn't ever listen to your **sixth sense**.
   a hunch

4) I look forward to **climbing the walls**.
   Frustrated

5) After you **straighten something up**, it looks terrible.
   tady

PART III It's Halftime

Students 1—2—3

Before you start the Halftime Activities, you must first complete pages 124-132 of Chapter 8. These activities are designed to get you to think about and discuss the meaning and use of the 15 expressions you have just studied.

■ **EXPRESSION GUIDE:** With your class, in small groups, or with friends, look over and talk about the idioms and slang you've been studying. Write down any extra information. Here are some questions to ask each other:

1) What kinds of people do you think use these expressions?
   (young, old, male, female...)

2) Where do you think you might hear these expressions?
   (school, beach, home, work, restaurant, nightclub, store...)

3) How do you think people say these expressions?
   (happy, angry, neutral, excited...)

EXPRESSION GUIDE

turn down	call it a day/night	lend a hand	wild *slang*	a shortcut
have time to kill	a bummer *slang*	luck out	get even	fish for compliments
sixth sense	get it	climb the walls *slang*	straighten up	tough

■ **CIRCLE AND DISCUSS** key words or phrases that show the meaning of the expression. It's best to work with a partner.

1) Karen beat Stefan playing darts five times in a row. Now he wants to keep playing to **get even** with her because he's such a poor sport.

2) Gary has a truck, so his friends always ask him to **lend them a hand** whenever they need some help moving.

3) Some people say that when that little voice inside you says something, it's important to listen because that's your **sixth sense** talking and it's usually right.

4) That is such **a bummer** that you didn't get to take the classes you wanted to take since they were full. You must be disappointed.

5) I can make great time getting to work now because the new freeway is open and I found another **shortcut** from one of the exits.

6) There are some coyotes near my house, so I've been keeping my cat inside, but he is **climbing the walls** wanting to go outside!

7) Murat is so happy he has done well in school that he doesn't care if people think he is **fishing for compliments** when he talks about it!

8) We offered to let Brad stay at our house until he found another place to live, but he **turned us down** because he wasn't sure how long it would take him. He's going to stay at his folks.

9) Joao and Rui decided to **straighten up** their garage. They had so much stuff in it that they couldn't park their car there anymore.

10) Carlos said climbing the Athabasca Glacier in Canada's magnificent British Columbia was one of **the wildest** things he has ever done.

11) Linda isn't used to **having time to kill** because she's normally too busy. I told her to go see lots of movies.

12) Oh no! You're going to **get it**. We just had the carpets washed and you spilled coffee again!

13) After happy hour, dinner, a movie, dancing and coffee, we finally **called it a night** and went home.

14) Wow! I got a great parking place! I **lucked out** today, especially with all this rain and all the things I have to carry.

15) Japanese is one of the **toughest** languages I've ever studied because of the complex writing system and the differences between male and female speech.

■ **FIND OUT** about some grammar points and additional meanings of some expressions. Consult the Grammar Guide in Appendix E on page 181 for more information.

1) turn down—**Turn** is one of the most highly idiomatic (phrasal) verbs in English. Sometimes the phrasal verbs have more than one meaning. For example, you studied that **turn down** means to reject, but you might already know that it can also mean to decrease the volume (or dim the lights). **Turn up** means the opposite: to make the sound louder. It also means to appear. **Turn on** and **turn off** are two more very common phrasal verbs that have two

meanings each. The most common meanings are to start (**turn on**) or stop (**turn off**). Likewise, people can feel excited (**turned on**) or disgusted (**turned off**). Look at the following examples and choose **up**, **down**, **on**, or **off**.

a) Ugh, that guy talks with his mouth full of food. He **turns me**_____.

b) The music is too loud. Would you **turn it**_____?

c) I can't find my watch. I hope it **turns**_____.

d) I can't see very well. Would you **turn the lights**_____.

2) straighten up—**Straighten up** means to make neat or clean, but it also means to behave properly. **Straighten out** is more commonly used in this sense, but it also means to resolve or clear up a misunderstanding. Read the examples and decide on the best definition.

a) Karim was very bad at school, but his teacher **straightened him out.**_____

b) I don't know who the messages are from, but I'll **straighten it out.**_____

3) get it—You just studied that **get it** means to be punished. In Chapter 3, you studied that **get** can also mean to understand. People commonly say "I get it" or ask "Do you get it?". Of course, **get** can also mean to obtain something! Explain the meanings of **get it** in the following sentences:

a) The teacher asked me if I **got it**, but I wasn't sure._____

b) Jenny went to the store for milk, but do you know if she **got it**?_____

4) get even—While **get even** means to seek revenge, **be even** means to be the same or tied. Complete the sentence below with **get even** or **be even**.

a) I lent her $50.00, and she paid me back. We_____.

b) I cut my hair myself. _____it_____in the back?

5) a bummer—The noun **a bummer** has a verb form: **bum someone out** and an adjective form: **be bummed out**. Fill in the blanks with the noun, verb, or adjective form.

a) That_____me_____that you can't come with us! What_____
_____. I bet you feel_____too.

■ **EXPRESSION LOG:** (1) Choose 10 expressions from this chapter to practice by writing original sentences, then (2) add two new expressions that you hear. Follow the New Expression Guide in Appendix A on page 159.

- Listen for the key words in the boxes below and number them as they are said.
- Write down the corresponding expression.
- How was it said? Happy___ Neutral___ Irritated___

# _____	# _____	# _____	# _____	# _____
challenges	**do nothing**	**scolded**	**flattery**	**your time will come**
Expression	Expression	Expression	Expression	Expression
_____	_____	_____	_____	_____
H__ N__ I__	H__ N__ I__	H__ N__ I__	H__ N__ I__	H__ N__ I__
# _____	# _____	# _____	# _____	# _____
decline	**tidy**	**hit the jackpot**	**turn in**	**fantastic**
Expression	Expression	Expression	Expression	Expression
_____	_____	_____	_____	_____
H__ N__ I__	H__ N__ I__	H__ N__ I__	H__ N__ I__	H__ N__ I__
# _____	# _____	# _____	# _____	# _____
a shame	**go nuts**	**pitch in**	**the way to go**	**deja-vu**
Expression	Expression	Expression	Expression	Expression
_____	_____	_____	_____	_____
H__ N__ I__	H__ N__ I__	H__ N__ I__	H__ N__ I__	H__ N__ I__

RULES: Roll the die and move ahead to the corresponding box. Mark your place by writing your name in the box. You should go around the board three times.

- If the number is below three, use the expression in the box in a **HAPPY** tone.
- If the number is over three, use the expression in the box in an **IRRITATED** tone.
- If the number is three, use the expression in the box in a **NEUTRAL** tone.

1. lend a hand	2. fish for compliments	3. straighten up	4. tough	5. have time to kill
names:	names:	names:	names:	names:
6. a bummer	7. climb the walls	8. luck out	9. get it	10. sixth sense
names:	names:	names:	names:	names:
11. turn down	12. call it a day/night	13. get even	14. a shortcut	15. spaced out
names:	names:	names:	names:	names:

lend a hand

CHAPTER

9

better late than never

count on

a sweetheart

for real

weird

turn in

have something wired

the works

fed up with

fill in

out in left field

creepy

have had it

wishy-washy

a blast

Student Group 1

Learn the meanings of five expressions by completing the following exercises. Work with Student Group 1 or by yourself.

■ **GUESS** the meanings of the five expressions.

1) You can count on Karl to pick you up at the airport. He'll be there.

2) My hair turned a weird shade of green when I was on the swim team.

3) I like baked potatoes with the works: butter, sour cream and chives.

4) It's past the deadline, but better late than never.

5) These shoes have had it. It's time for a new pair.

■ **CHECK OUT** the definitions and examples of the expressions.

1) count on—depend on, trust.
   You can always count on Pasta Cucina for good Italian food.

2) weird—strange, unnatural, sometimes fantastic.
   All of a sudden my car started to make a weird sound. I'd better take it to the mechanics to get it checked out.

3) the works—including everything.
   Her new system has a subwoofer, a video card, and cable modem—the works.

4) better late than never—it's not too late to do something.
   He's 75, but he's learning to dance! Better late than never!

5) have had it—not be useful anymore.
   My tires have had it. I better get some new ones.

■ **QUICK FIX**—Match the expressions to the words that are similar.

1) worn out   _4_ better late than never

2) rely   _3_ the works

3) all the extras   _5_ weird

4) act after the appropriate time   _|_ have had it

5) bizarre   _2_ count on

■ **CLOZE IT**—Use one of the above expressions to complete the sentences. Be sure to check your grammar!

1) You can still apologize. _Better late that never_.

2) This meat smells _weird_. I think it must be old. We'd better not eat it.

3) This printer _has had it_. The paper keeps getting jammed in it.

4) Give me _the works_ on my hamburger.

5) Don't _count on_ him for help. He's too busy.

■ **SENSE OR NONSENSE**—With your classmates, discuss the sentences and decide if they do or don't make sense.

1) Death Valley, the lowest point in in the United States, is a very **weird** place. _S_

2) You can **count on** a brain to figure the problem out. _S_

3) Give me **the works**—nothing extra. _NS_

4) I don't need new jeans because these **have had it**. _NS_

5) She finally understands! **Better late than never**! _S_

■ **PLUG IT IN**—Use the expressions to replace the underlined words. Make sure to check your grammar! Check the Index/Glossary for words you may not know.

1) This wallet is wearing out. I'd better get a new one.
has had it

2) Take your time doing this. Don't worry about how long it takes.
Better late than never

3) My stomach felt a little strange after I ate that junk food. _weird_

4) We decided to get all the accessories for our new entertainment center.
the works

5) I'll be there for you.
Can count on me

Student Group 2

Learn the meanings of the following five expressions by completing the exercises. Work with Student Group 2 or by yourself.

■ **GUESS** the meanings of the five expressions.

[handwritten: ven asia me. demelo ami]

1) We have to **turn in** our homework on Tuesday.

[handwritten: cumbiar de opinion]

2) I'm so **wishy-washy** today. I can't decide if I want Thai food or Vietnamese food.

[handwritten: dar buenas ideas. o malas ideas]

3) Don't ask him. He is **out in left field**. He won't know.

[handwritten: lla estoy cansado de Ti o disgustado]

4) I'm **fed up with** all this work. I'm going to take a break.

[handwritten: sweet person: buena persona corazon y dulce amuble]

5) Thank you so much. You're such **a sweetheart** for helping me.

■ **CHECK OUT** the definitions and examples of the expressions.

1) **turn in**—give something such as homework to a teacher or a report to a boss, hand in.
   I have to turn in this proposal on Thursday.

2) **wishy-washy**—can't decide, difficulty in making up one's mind.
   After five years together, he still doesn't know if he wants to marry her. What a wishy-washy guy.

3) **out in left field**—have strange ideas, be very mistaken or wrong.
   You think we should pay more taxes! You're really out in left field.

4) **fed up with**—very tired of something, very bored or disgusted.
   Sonia finally got fed up with his lies, so she broke up with him.

5) **a sweetheart**—a kind, thoughtful, giving person.
   Louise is really a sweetheart for organizing this surprise party.

■ **QUICK FIX**—Match the expressions to the words that are similar.

1) crazy   _3_ turn in *[handwritten: darle algo a alguien]*

2) kind   _1_ out in left field *[handwritten: estar loco]*

3) deliver   _4_ fed up with

4) can't tolerate   _5_ wishy-washy *[handwritten: cumbiar de opinion]*

5) can't choose   _2_ a sweetheart *[handwritten: mi novia persona dulce]*
   [handwritten: can't shus]

■ **CLOZE IT**—Use one of the above expressions to complete the sentences. Be sure to check your grammar!

1) Our neighbor is _a sweetheart_ for keeping an eye on our house.

2) Dean got _fed up with_ his job, so he found a better one.

3) Liz never knows if she wants to join us or not. She's so _wishy washy_

4) Can you believe what Kathy thinks we should do? She's totally _out left field_

5) We were swamped, but we _turned in_ the assignment on time!

■ **SENSE OR NONSENSE**—With your classmates, discuss the sentences and decide if they do or don't make sense.

1) **Wishy-washy** people make great parents. _NS_

2) Going out with **a sweetheart** is usually a good thing. _S_

3) It's easy to stick with it if you're **fed up**. _NS_

4) If you make good time, you can usually **turn things in** on time. _S_

5) People who are closed-minded may also be **out in left field**. _S_

■ **PLUG IT IN**—Use the expressions to replace the underlined words. Make sure to check your grammar! Check the Index/Glossary for words you may not know.

1) Linda will be able to <u>hand deliver</u> this letter to the president.
   turn in

2) I <u>cannot put up with</u> your jerky behavior anymore.
   fed up with

3) That was so nice of you to give us this beautiful gift. You're <u>a dear</u>.
   sweet heart

4) Jennifer <u>really lives in another world</u> when it comes to handling money.
   out in lestt field

5) Please make up your mind and don't <u>change it again</u>.
   wishy - washy

Student Group 3

Learn the meanings of the following five expressions by completing the exercises. Work with Student Group 3 or by yourself.

■ **GUESS** the meanings of the five expressions..

1) You're flying here for the holidays? For real?

2) Ugh, this place is creepy. Let's get out of here.

3) You need to fill in all the blanks on this form.

4) We had a blast on our vacation in Hawaii. You have to go there sometime!

5) Jason has practiced so much that he has it wired.

■ **CHECK OUT** the definitions and examples of the expressions.

1) for real—seriously, not kidding, genuine.
   He is going to quit his job? For real?

2) creepy—strange, bizarre, uncomfortable, scary.
   Wow, that is a creepy story. I don't know if I'll be able to sleep tonight.

3) fill in—complete, give information to someone.
   If you miss class, I'll fill you in on what happened.

4) a blast—a great, wonderful time.
   My conversation class is a blast! I love it!

5) have something wired—be able to do something really well, successfully.
   I have this class wired. I'm definitely getting an A.

■ **QUICK FIX**—Match the expressions to the words that are similar.

1) inform   _3_ creepy

2) good at   _1_ fill in

3) frightening   _2_ have something wired

4) true   _5_ a blast

5) fun   _4_ for real

■ **CLOZE IT**—Use one of the above expressions to complete the sentences. Be sure to check your grammar!

1) Are you _for real_____, or are you just kidding me?

2) How _creepy_____ that you dreamed that. You must feel really spaced out.

3) The class was easy. I'll _hfill_____ it you _win_____ later.

4) Don't worry. I know what I'm doing. I _have it wired_____.

5) We had _a blast_____ at the concert last night. It was awesome!

■ **SENSE OR NONSENSE**—With your classmates, discuss the sentences and decide if they do or don't make sense.

1) Fake people are always **for real**. _No_

2) I can do this with my eyes closed because I **have it wired**. _S_

3) All my friends came to the party and we had **a blast**. _S_

4) It's fun to hang out with **creepy** people. _NS_

5) He **filled me in** with all the information about the meeting that I missed. _S_

■ **PLUG IT IN**—Use the expressions to replace the underlined words. Make sure to check your grammar! Check the Index/Glossary for words you may not know.

1) My boyfriend and I had a great time riding his motorcycle in the mountains.
   a blast

2) That old man who hangs out in the park is very bizarre.
   creepy

3) Marc is really a doctor? Are you pulling my leg?
   for real

4) Tom can design anything because it's like second nature to him.
   have something wired

5) Would you let me know what takes place here while I'm on vacation?
   filling in on

Questions to Ask Someone from Student Group 1

Ask Student 1 the following questions. He or she will tell you the answers. You should write down the answers. Student 1 can look at pages 140-141 to find the answers.

■ **TELL ME:** Ask Student 1 the following questions to get the expressions.

1) What is another way to say something is strange?_____

2) If I want everything on my sandwich, what can I say?_____

3) How can I describe something that is no longer useful?_____

4) What is another way to say you can depend on someone?_____

5) Is there a way to say it's not too late?_____

■ **MAKE THIS MAKE SENSE:** Ask Student 1 to change these sentences to make sense.

1) It's not easy to trust people you can **count on**.

2) You're not going to give it a shot? **Better late than never**. Good for you.

3) These speakers sound great. They**'ve had it**.

4) I want **the works**, so don't give me any pickles or onions on my hotdog.

5) I didn't feel **weird** when I got food poisoning and threw up.

Questions to Ask Someone from Student Group 2

Ask Student 2 the following questions. He or she will tell you the answers. You should write down the answers. Student 2 can look at pages 142-143 to find the answers.

■ **TELL ME:** Ask Student 2 the following questions to get the expressions.

1) What is a way to say you can't decide?_____

2) Is there an expression which means you can't tolerate something anymore? _____

3) What can I call someone who is really nice and generous?_____

4) If I have to give my homework to my teacher, what can I say?_____

5) Is there a way to say someone is really crazy?_____

■ **MAKE THIS MAKE SENSE:** Ask Student 2 to change these sentences to make sense.

1) People who are **out in left field** are good employees.

2) If I **turn something in**, I keep it for myself.

3) When you are **fed up with** someone, you want to hang out with them.

4) It's easy to choose a ring if you are **wishy-washy**.

5) It's difficult to get along with **a sweetheart**.

Questions to Ask Someone from Student Group 3

Ask Student 3 the following questions. He or she will tell you the answers. You should write down the answers. Student 3 can look at pages 144-145 to find the answers.

■ **TELL ME:** Ask Student 3 following questions to get the expressions.

1) What is a way to say something is frightening?_____

2) Is there another expression that means to have a lot of fun?_____

3) If you can do something extremely well, what can you say?_____

4) How can I say something is serious or genuine?_____

5) What do you say if you need to complete something?_____

■ **MAKE THIS MAKE SENSE:** Ask Student 3 to change these sentences to make sense.

1) Students usually don't have to **fill in** blanks on traditional quizzes.

2) It's **a blast** to do laundry all weekend.

3) If you **have something wired**, it's hard for you to do.

4) **Creepy** movies are good for the whole family.

5) You shouldn't trust someone who is **for real**.

Students 1—2—3

Before you start the Halftime Activities, you must first complete pages 140-148 of Chapter 9. These activities are designed to get you to think about and discuss the meaning and use of the 15 expressions you have just studied.

■ **EXPRESSION GUIDE:** With your class, in small groups, or with friends, look over and talk about the idioms and slang you've been studying. Write down any extra information. Here are some questions to ask each other:

1) What kinds of people do you think use these expressions?
(young, old, male, female...)

2) Where do you think you might hear these expressions?
(school, beach, home, work, restaurant, nightclub, store...)

3) How do you think people say these expressions
(happy, angry, neutral, excited...)

EXPRESSION GUIDE

count on	weird	the works	better late than never	have had it
a sweetheart	turn in	fed up with	out in left field *slang*	wishy-washy
for real	have something wired *slang*	fill in	creepy	a blast *slang*

■ **CIRCLE AND DISCUSS** key words or phrases that show the meaning of the expression. It's best to work with a partner.

1) We want **the works** on our pizza: sausage, pepperoni, ham, onions, olives, peppers, mushrooms and extra cheese.

2) What are all those **creepy** noises? This is the second week we've heard these bizarre sounds in the middle of the night.

3) John was such **a sweetheart** to bring me over chicken soup and my favorite magazines when I was sick in bed last week.

4) They're having **a blast** studying English in San Diego. They're made lots of new friends from all over the world, they've visited San Francisco and Los Angeles, and they've been body boarding at the beach! Plus, they've learned a lot of English!

5) Paul is **out in left field** when it comes to understanding his employees because he doesn't listen to them. No wonder everyone keeps quitting.

6) This bed **has had it**. It's way too soft and it sinks down in the middle. My back has been killing me! It's time to get a new one.

7) Everyone has to **turn in** their requests for vacation time by the end of the month.

8) Matthew **has fixing cars wired**. His Dad is a mechanic, and he grew up watching him repair cars.

9) You can always **count on** Verna to listen to you. She'll always give you good advice too, because she is a very fair person, and she knows how to use her sixth sense.

10) My little five-year-old keeps asking me if Santa Claus is **for real**. I don't want to tell him the truth yet because I want him to enjoy using his imagination.

11) It's the day after his birthday, and I forgot to get him a present. I'm going shopping right now! **Better late than never!**

12) I can't decide whether to take that job or not. My current job is good, but this job might be better. I'm really **wishy-washy** about it.

13) That is so **weird**! I just saw that book on my desk two seconds ago, but now I don't know where it is. Have you seen it?

14) We are really **fed up with** our working conditions. We're overworked. We work about 50 hours a week. And we're underpaid. We get a .5% raise a year. It's terrible.

15) You have to **fill in** this form very carefully. If there are any mistakes, they won't process it.

■ **FIND OUT** about some grammar points and additional meanings of some expressions. Consult the Grammar Guide in Appendix E on page 181 for more information.

1) **turn in**—As you studied in Chapter 8, **turn** is a very idiomatic verb. **Turn in** has another meaning in addition to the one you studied. **Turn out** has two meanings also. Read the sentences below and match the meanings to the definitions.

a) The food **turned out** delicious.___	**1)** go to sleep
b) I'm tired. It's time to **turn in**.___	**2)** show up, come
c) A lot of people **turned out** for the concert.___	**3)** result

2) **fill in**—This phrasal verb also has another common meaning, which is to take the place or substitute for someone. **Fill out** also means to complete some information, usually on a form. **Fill in** the blanks below with **in** or **out**.

   a) Here is your driver's license application. Be sure to fill it_____completely.

   b) Nancy is sick today, so Kate is filling_____for her.

   c) I missed the first hour. Would you fill me_____on what was said?

3) **have had it**—This expression can also mean **fed up with**. Explain the meaning of the following examples of **have had it**:

   a) I've had it with this stupid photocopy machine. Meaning:_____

   b) This stupid photocopy machine has had it. Meaning:_____

4) **for real**—**Get real** and **real** are two more common expressions, but the meanings are different. Read the situations below and decide what you they mean:

   a) Come on! You can't change people! **Get real**! Meaning:_____

   b) Carlos is a **real** prince. He's the best guy I've ever met.
   Meaning:_____

5) **a sweetheart**—**Sweetheart** is also an expression of intimacy between men and women and parents and children. **Sweetie, sweetypie, honey**, and **darling** can also be used in the same way as **sweetheart**. BUT sometimes it is rude to call someone who you don't know **a sweetheart**, so be careful using these words. Look at the possibilities below and write OK if you can use any of these expressions.

a)	mother to son:_____	*e)*	friend to friend:_____
b)	employee to boss:_____	*f)*	student to teacher:_____
c)	man to woman in bar:_____	*g)*	person to police officer:_____
d)	customer to waitress:_____	*h)*	boyfriend to girlfriend:_____

6) **creepy**—The adjective **creepy** has a verb phrase counterpart: **give someone the creeps**. Complete the sentence below with the correct form of **creepy**.

   a) I don't like this_____ place because it_____.

7) **killer**—The adjective **killer** has a verb counterpart which has several meanings. Following are three examples. Match them to their definitions.

a) This guy **kills** me. He's so funny.___	**1)** can't believe
b) Let's **kill** the pizza.___	**2)** cracks me up
c) It's **kills** me how lazy he is.___	**3)** finish

■ **EXPRESSION LOG:** (1) Choose 10 expressions from this chapter to practice by writing original sentences, then (2) add two new expressions that you hear. Follow the New Expression Guide in Appendix A on page 159.

Each of the following expressions will be used to write a response to the questions you hear. Instructions:
- Listen to the questions and choose an expression to use in your answer.
- Listen to the questions again and write a complete response using the expression.
- You will have one minute to write each sentence.
- After all the questions are asked, you can go back to check your responses.

wishy-washy	out in left field	turn in	creepy	a sweetheart
count on	a blast	for real	fill in	the works
have had it	fed up with	better late than never	have something wired	weird

EXPRESSION   RESPONSE

1)	
2)	
3)	
4)	
5)	
6)	
7)	
8)	
9)	
10)	
11)	
12)	
13)	
14)	
15)	

RULES: Double Dice.
- Roll the die and go to the corresponding box.
- Roll the die again. If the number is:
  - ODD (1,3,5) use the expression in a positive tone.
  - EVEN (2,4,6) use the expression in a negative tone.
- Go around the board three times. Mark your place by writing your names.

s) count on	r) fill in	q) have some-thing wired	p) say anything	o) weird
names:	names:	names:	names:	names:
j) creepy	k) have had it	l) a blast	m) turn in	n) the works
names:	names:	names:	names:	names:
i) a sweetheart	h) say anything	g) miss a turn	f) wishy-washy	e) out in left field
names:	names:	names:	names:	names:
Start	a) fed up with	b) better late than never	c) for real	d) skip a turn
	names:	names:	names:	names:

"I Spy"
Group A

INSTRUCTIONS: (Group B turn to page 157)
- GROUP A: Look at the list of expressions below.
- GROUP B will describe 10 of the expressions to you. You must identify which expressions Group B describes. You will number the expressions #1 - #10 in the order that you hear them. Also, circle the letter B.
- When you think you know the expression, you must say "I spy" to see if you are correct. Then number the expression.
- If you are correct, you have to use the target expression in a sentence. Your sentence must be correct, so be sure to check with your group. Group B will decide if they like your sentences, so make them interesting!

turn in #___ A or B	weird #___ A or B	drop off #___ A or B	back in a flash #___ A or B
get even #___ A or B	call it a day #___ A or B	wild #___ A or B	fish for compliments #___ A or B
step on it #___ A or B	for real #___ A or B	nosy #___ A or B	have had it #___ A or B
a chicken #___ A or B	hot #___ A or B	a blast #___ A or B	out in left field #___ A or B
loaded #___ A or B	hit the sack #___ A or B	straighten up #___ A or B	turn down #___ A or B
a knockout #___ A or B	put one's foot in one's mouth #___ A or B	fill in #___ A or B	the works #___ A or B

Dialogue Match
Partner A

- Partner A: Begin the dialogue. Read your first line to Partner B.
- Partner B: Turn to page 157 for your half of the dialogue.
- NUMBER the exchanges 1, 3, 5, 7, 9, 11.

___ Hey, **better late than never**. I can show you a few **shortcuts.**, but I'm sure you'll **come up with** your own strategies too.

___ You might **luck out**. Guessing is sometimes a great strategy. Just don't get too **fed up with** your class. Try to keep an open-mind and remember what **a brain** you are.

___ Yeah, I know. Studying for the TOEFL can be **tough**, but you'll **work it out**. I can **lend you a hand** studying if you'd like.

___ Hey, what's the matter with you today? You look really **bummed out**.

___ No problem, I know I can **count on** you too. When do you want to get together?

___ Well, you'll have to learn to use your **sixth sense**. Sometimes you just know what the answer is. Don't second guess yourself.

a chicken

"I Spy"
Group B

INSTRUCTIONS:
- **Group B:** Look at the list of expressions below. Choose any 10 to describe to Group A. Number the expressions that you choose #1 - #10 and circle the letter B.
- When Group A thinks they know the answer, they must shout out "I spy." Tell Group A if they are correct. If they are correct, they must make a sentence using the expression.
- Your group will decide if Group A has made a good and interesting sentence.

turn in #___ A or B	**weird** #___ A or B	**drop off** #___ A or B	**back in a flash** #___ A or B
get even #___ A or B	**call it a day** #___ A or B	**wild** #___ A or B	**fish for compliments** #___ A or B
step on it #___ A or B	**for real** #___ A or B	**nosy** #___ A or B	**have had it** #___ A or B
a chicken #___ A or B	**hot** #___ A or B	**a blast** #___ A or B	**out in left field** #___ A or B
loaded #___ A or B	**hit the sack** #___ A or B	**straighten up** #___ A or B	**turn down** #___ A or B
a knockout #___ A or B	**put one's foot in one's mouth** #___ A or B	**fill in** #___ A or B	**the works** #___ A or B

Dialogue Match
Partner B

- Listen to Partner A begin a conversation. What will you say next?
- **NUMBER the exchanges in the order they should be said 2, 4, 6, 8, 10, 12.**

___ You're right. Maybe I'll **luck out** and guess the right answers.

___ That would be great. I know that you **have the TOEFL wired**, but the test is in a few days. Do you really **have time to kill** in the next few days?

___ I **am bummed out**. I'm **climbing the walls** in my TOEFL class. Some of it is really **tough**. I just don't **get it**.

___ Hmm, let me see. How about...

___ I hope so. I get so spaced out sometimes in class. I'm so **wishy-washy** about choosing an answer.

___ Well, I'm not **a brain** at English like you are, but I'll give it a shot. You're **a sweetheart** for offering to help me.

Grand Finale

Work with one or two partners to write a dialogue or a story using a minimum of 2 expressions from Chapters 7-8-9 and from your Expression Logs. There is no maximum, so use as many expressions as possible! Your teacher may announce winners!

the works

NEW EXPRESSION GUIDE

TV/Music/Radio/Movies/Friends/Acquaintances/Strangers/Newspapers/
Magazines/School/Beach/Restaurants/Clubs/Stores/Gym

Use this Guide to find new expressions to record in your Expression Log. Answer the following questions the best you can:

1. WHAT_____
   What is the expression?

2. WHO_____
   Who said it? (male, female, young, old...type of person—business person, student, worker, boss...)

3. WHERE_____
   Where did you hear it? (place, location, time...)

4. HOW_____
   How was it said? (friendly, formally, angry, funny, neutral...)

5. MEANING_____
   What do you think it means? It's OK if you don't know, but ask someone!

6. SAMPLE SENTENCE_____
   _____

NEW EXPRESSIONS LIST

Use this page to keep track of all the new expressions that you record in you Expression Log.

Expression	Meaning
1.	
2.	
3.	
4.	
5.	
6.	
7.	
8.	
9.	
10.	
11.	
12.	
13.	
14.	
15.	
16.	
17.	
18.	
19.	
20.	
21.	
22.	
23.	
24.	
25.	
26.	
27.	
28.	
29.	
30.	

ANSWER KEY

CHAPTER 1

Part I

Student 1 - pg. 2

■ **Quick Fix**
1) 3
2) 1
3) 5
4) 2
5) 4

■ **Sense or Nonsense**
1) S
2) NS
3) NS
4) NS
5) S

Student 2 - p. 4

■ **Quick Fix**
1) 4
2) 5
3) 1
4) 2
5) 3

■ **Sense or Nonsense**
1) NS
2) NS
3) S
4) NS
5) S

Student 3 - p. 6

■ **Quick Fix**
1) 3
2) 1
3) 5
4) 2
5) 4

■ **Cloze It**
1) check out
2) no big deal
3) grab a bite
4) nuts about
5) bucks

■ **Plug In**
1) nuts about
2) It's no big deal
3) grab a bite at
4) check out
5) bucks

■ **Cloze It**
1) jerk
2) kidding
3) awesome
4) cracks (us) up
5) cross our fingers, keep our fingers crossed

■ **Plug In**
1) cracking up
2) will cross my fingers
3) jerk
4) awesome
5) kidding

■ **Cloze It**
1) Hang out
2) buddies
3) feels like
4) cool
5) am broke

■ **Sense or Nonsense**
1) S
2) S
3) NS
4) S
5) NS

Part II

Student 1 - p. 8

■ **Tell Me**

1) no big deal

2) bucks

3) nuts about

4) grab a bite

5) check out

Student 2 - p. 9

■ **Tell Me**

1) I'm kidding

2) awesome
3) cross your fingers
4) crack up
5) a jerk

Student 3 - p. 10

■ **Tell Me**

1) hang out
2) cool

3) a buddy

4) feel like
5) I'm broke

■ **Plug In**
1) feels like
2) hang out
3) buddies
4) are broke
5) cool

■ **Make This Make Sense
(possible answers)**
1) I WANT to hang out with him...
2) ...you WILL check out new places
3) It's A VERY BIG DEAL that you...
4) ...WORK.
5) We usually grab a bite for BREAKFAST.

■ **Make This Make Sense
(possible answers)**
1) ...that you WILL get that job...
2) ...Tom is so SILLY that...
3) ...it is so FUNNY
4) ...he is such a good guy.
5) ...is a really BORING way...

■ **Make This Make Sense
(possible answers)**
1) I ALWAYS feel like...
2) ...We met each other in elementary school.
3) ...so he CAN'T buy anything in cash.
4) It IS FUN to hang out...
5) John Travolta SEEMS like a cool guy.

Part III

CIRCLE AND DISCUSS – p. 12

1) not enough time for breakfast or lunch, only 15 minutes, (grab a bite)
2) What? can't believe, that's nuts (kidding)
3) haven't been out for a long time (feel like)
4) always together, holding hands, giggling, making goo-goo eyes (nuts about)
5) since they were kids, they still play every week (buddies)
6) if we get, we'll win (keep your fingers crossed)
7) new shopping center, to see what's there (check out)
8) waterfalls, Yosemite, after it rains (awesome)
9) drink, after they work out (hang out)
10) don't worry (no big deal)
11) invited Tina, she wouldn't stay because she didn't like his house (jerk)
12) always loaded with cash, treats everyone (bucks)
13) can't go, too expensive (broke)
14) funniest, faces he can make (crack up)
15) new offices, new furniture, new computer, better phone system (cool)

FIND OUT - p. 13

1e) We check it out last weekend.
2b) She thinks Kevin is a crack up.
3a) another cup of coffee   **b)** going to the pool
4c) George is nuts to sail to Hawaii without any experience!
5c) I'm not kidding!   **d)** No kidding!
6a) no   **b)** no   **c)** no
7b) friendly   **c)** unfriendly

Part IV

TUNE IN - p. 15

1) awesome	6) crack up	11) grab a bite
2) cross your fingers	7) hang out	12) kidding
3) feel like	8) nuts about	13) no big deal
4) check out	9) jerk	14) be broke
5) buddy	10) bucks	15) cool

CHAPTER 2

Part I

Student 1 - p. 20

■ **Quick Fix**
1) 2
2) 4
3) 5
4) 1
5) 3

■ **Cloze It**
1) bugs
2) no pain, no gain
3) jock
4) classy
5) give up

■ **Sense or Nonsense**
1) S
2) NS
3) S
4) NS
5) S

■ **Plug In**
1) a jock
2) classy
3) bugs me
4) no pain, no gain
5) give up

Student 2 - p. 22

■ **Quick Fix**
1) 5
2) 2
3) 4
4) 3
5) 1

■ **Cloze It**
1) went blank
2) show off
3) a nerd
4) laid-back
5) Never mind

■ **Sense or Nonsense**
1) NS
2) NS
3) S
4) NS
5) S

■ **Plug In**
1) show off
2) laid-back
3) never mind
4) am going blank
5) nerd

Student 3 - p. 24

■ **Quick Fix**
1) 5
2) 3
3) 4
4) 1
5) 2

■ **Cloze It**
1) kick back
2) is falling for
3) am beat
4) can't stand
5) money to burn

■ **Sense or Nonsense**
1) T
2) F
3) T
4) T
5) F

■ **Plug In**
1) money to burn
2) is falling for
3) beat
4) kick back
5) can't stand

Part II

Student 1 - p. 26

■ **Tell Me**

1) no pain, no gain

2) give up

3) a jock

4) classy

■ **Make This Make Sense (possible answers)**

1) It WOULD bug me A LOT if you played...

2) You SHOULD NOT give up eating healthy food...

3) If you WANT to get more money,...

4) A Mercedes Benz IS a classy car.

5) bug

5) Typical jocks ARE NOT interested in literature...

14) I just remembered (never mind)

15) anyone who hurts kids, elderly, animals (can't stand)

Student 2 - p. 27

■ **Tell Me**

1) show off

2) a nerd

3) go blank

4) laid-back

5) never mind

■ **Make This Make Sense (possible answers)**

1) ...computer nerd. He ALWAYS spends on his...

2) I SOMETIMES go blank...

3) Never mind. I DON'T really need your help.

4) ...She NEVER shows off.

5) Bella is so laid-back that she NEVER loses...

Student 3 - p. 28

■ **Tell Me**

1) beat

2) fall for someone

3) can't stand

4) money to burn

5) kick back

■ **Make This Make Sense (possible answers)**

1) ...money to burn that I CAN go out for ...

2) ...eating spinach, so let's NOT have ANY for...

3) Most men LOVE to kick back...

4) Matty is so beat that she ISN'T going to go...

5) ...because she is such a SWEET PERSON.

Part III

CIRCLE AND DISCUSS - p. 30

1) he wants to see her every day (fall for someone)

2) nice but, loves talking about it all the time (nerd)

3) not going to, already worked too hard, almost finished (give up)

4) five long messages, with giving me a chance (bug)

5) treated his whole class to sushi (money to burn)

6) sorry, give me a second to remember (go blank)

7) even when there are people, he wants to watch sports (jock)

8) he can spin, jump, fly (show off)

9) at home, read the paper, rented videos, played cards and darts (kick back)

10) cool, easy-going, friendly (laid-back)

11) new hotel casino in Las Vegas...rivals Cesar's Palace (classy)

12) falling asleep standing up (beat)

13) worked every day for four months straight to finish (no pain, no gain)

FIND OUT - pp. 30-31

1c) virus or bacteria

2c) can't be beat

3b) He's fooling her!

4a) nerdy, nerd

5a) a show-off, shows off

6a) gerund   **b)** noun

Part IV

TUNE IN - p. 32

1) give up - Y   **2)** show off - Y

3) kick back - N   **4)** be beat - N

5) a nerd - N   **6)** no pain, no gain - Y

7) never mind - N   **8)** be classy - N

9) bug someone - N   **10)** go blank - Y

11) a jock - Y   **12)** laid-back - Y

13) can't stand - Y   **14)** fall for someone - Y

15) money to burn - Y

CHAPTER 3

Part I

Student 1 - p. 36

■ **Quick Fix**

1) 4

2) 3

3) 1

4) 5

5) 2

■ **Cloze It**

1) is dressed to kill

2) a slob

3) ripped it off

4) get with it

5) I bet

■ **Sense or Nonsense**

1) NS

2) S

3) NS

4) S

5) NS

■ **Plug In**

1) get with it

2) got/was dressed to kill

3) rip off

4) a slob

5) I bet

Student 2 - p. 38

■ **Quick Fix**

1) 4

2) 5

3) 1

4) 3

5) 2

■ **Cloze It**

1) blow it

2) is so swamped

3) Cut it out

4) goof off/around

5) junk food

■ **Sense or Nonsense**

1) S

■ **Plug In**

1) are swamped

2) S
3) NS
4) NS
5) S

Student 3 - p. 40

■ **Quick Fix**
1) 3
2) 5
3) 4
4) 1
5) 2

■ **Sense or Nonsense**
1) NS
2) NS
3) NS
4) NS
5) S

Part II

Student 1 - p. 42

■ **Tell Me**

1) dressed to kill

2) get with it

3) I bet

4) rip off

5) a slob

Part II

Student 2 - p. 43

■ **Tell Me**

1) blow it

2) cut it out

3) goof off/around

4) junk food

5) I'm swamped

---

2) junk food
3) Cut it out
4) blow it
5) goof around/off

■ **Cloze It**
1) hit the books
2) big heads
3) puts anyone down
4) is bogus
5) fixed me up

■ **Plug In**
1) a big head
2) puts down
3) is bogus
4) fixed us up
5) hit the books

■ **Make This Make Sense (possible answers)**

1) I DIDN'T get ripped off when I only paid $7.00...

2) You'd better get with it now, so DON'T take...

3) Young single people OFTEN get dressed to kill...

4) Gustavo is such a slob because he NEVER cleans...

5) I bet you ARE upset about...

■ **Make This Make Sense (possible answers)**

1) I HATE it when you yell at me, so cut it out!

2) Let's get started...by NOT goofing around.

3) I'm so glad I DIDN'T blow my test.

4) She's so swamped that she CAN'T go to the...

5) I want to be healthy, so I'm NOT going to eat...

Student 3 - p. 44

■ **Tell Me**

1) have a big head

2) put down

3) fix me up

4) it's bogus

5) hit the books

■ **Make This Make Sense (possible answers)**

1) It's NOT fun to be fixed up with a jerk.

2) I DON'T need to hit the books...

3) Jack is a very INSINCERE person...

4) I DON'T like to hang out with people who...

5) It's bogus that my new car DOESN'T run...

Part III

CIRCLE AND DISCUSS - p. 46
1) Be careful of "get rich quick" (bogus)
2) tourists, don't know how things work, paying too much (rip off)
3) If you want, actor, audition, won't get the part (blow it)
4) Jody and Doug, They went out to dinner, Oh well (fix someone up)
5) If we want to win, practice hard every day (get with it)
6) eat, in the afternoon, lot of work to do, don't feel so great (junk food)
7) kids, nerdy, funny looking, not so smart (put down)
8) you worked every day, you're beat (I bet)
9) move into a new house, too busy to go out (swamped)
10) have to prepare, get ready (hit the books)
11) never invites anyone to his house, messy (a slob)
12) tickling, I can't breathe (cut it out)
13) became the boss, kiss the ground she walks on (have a big head)
14) get a lot of attention   (dressed to kill)
15) not doing their work, surfing the net, reading e-mail (goof around)

FIND OUT - p. 47
1a) advertisements, mail you don't really need
 b) a car that doesn't run well
 c) stuff, things you don't really need
2a) able to   **b)** understand
3a) lose his temper   **b)** waste money
4a) of course, sure   **b)** no problem, you're welcome
5a) Put it down!   **b)** a put-down
6a) arrange for you to   **b)** repair
     have a car
7a) 3 - noun   **b)** 1 - active   **c)** 2 - passive

Part IV

TUNE IN - p. 49
1) a big head
2) get with it
3) goof off
4) rip off
5) swamped
6) a slob
7) dressed to kill
8) blow it
9) cut it out
10) hit the books
11) bogus
12) I bet
13) put down
14) fix someone up
15) junk food

CHAPTER 4

Part I

Student 1 - p. 56

■ **Quick Fix**
1) 2
2) 4
3) 5
4) 1
5) 3

■ **Cloze It**
1) get over
2) looking forward to
3) in the same boat
4) down-to-earth
5) a backseat driver

■ **Sense or Nonsense**
1) NS
2) S
3) NS
4) S
5) NS

■ **Plug In**
1) are looking forward to it
2) down-to-earth
3) in the same boat
4) is still getting over
5) a backseat driver

Student 2 - p. 58

■ **Quick Fix**
1) 4
2) 3
3) 2
4) 5
5) 1

■ **Cloze It**
1) a sweet tooth
2) get together
3) Hang on
4) in hot water
5) seeing each other

■ **Sense or Nonsense**
1) NS
2) S
3) NS
4) NS
5) S

■ **Plug In**
1) have a sweet tooth
2) saw each other
3) in hot water
4) get together
5) hang on

Student 3 - p. 60

■ **Quick Fix**
1) 2
2) 3
3) 5
4) 4
5) 1

■ **Cloze It**
1) a shot
2) open-minded
3) made good time
4) go through
5) blind date

■ **Sense or Nonsense**
1) S
2) NS
3) S
4) S
5) NS

■ **Plug In**
1) give surfing a shot
2) We made good time.
3) go through
4) open-minded
5) Blind dates

Part II

Student 1 - p. 62

■ **Tell Me**
1) in the same boat
2) get over
3) down-to-earth
4) look forward to
5) a backseat driver

■ **Make This Make Sense (possible answers)**
1) I'm NOT looking forward to...
2) I DON'T enjoy...
3) It's DIFFICULT to...
4) I KNOW how you feel...
5) ...make me COMFORTABLE.

Student 2 - p. 63

■ **Tell Me**
1) get together
2) hang on
3) a sweet tooth
4) in hot water
5) see someone

■ **Make This Make Sense (possible answers)**
1) I MIND hanging on...
2) ...I love to eat CHOCOLATE.
3) I CAN'T STAND getting...
4) It's VERY fun...
5) I WILL get in hot water...

Student 3 - p. 64

■ **Tell Me**
1) make good time
2) go through
3) blind date
4) open-minded
5) give it a shot

■ **Make This Make Sense (possible answers)**
1) ...with CLOSED-MINDED people.
2) It's VERY easy...
3) ...I WILL try it!
4) A blind dates is ONE way to...
5) We DON'T make good time...

Part III

CIRCLE AND DISCUSS - pp. 65-66
1) chewed up, broke (in hot water)
2) hanging out, feel comfortable (down-to-earth)
3) First, Then, Finally (go through)
4) a month break, visit the Grand Canyon, (look forward to)
5) finished before I thought, can kick back (make good time)

6) so do I, neither do I, I do too (in the same boat)

7) chocolate chip cookie, M&Ms (a sweet tooth)

8) don't have all the experience, have some experience (give it a shot)

9) for three months, still haven't said, love (see each other)

10) two months, most of the injuries, one year, recover (get over)

11) nervous, had never seen each other (blind date)

12) two more weeks, find out why (hang on)

13) not used to so much traffic, make you nervous (backseat driver)

14) keep in touch, let me know (get together)

15) international, smart, easy to get along with (open-minded)

FIND OUT - pp. 66-67

1)a) 4   **b)** 1   **c)** 2   **d)** 3

2)a) gerund **b)** noun   **c)** gerund

3)a) noun - a get together

   b) verb - are getting together

   c) gerund (object) - getting together

4) someone who drives too slowly

5) Hang in there. They're leaving soon. Be patient!

6)a) bad   **b)** closed

Part IV

TUNE IN - p. 69

1) (look) **looking forward to - no** - studying all weekend, three tests

2) **in the same boat - yes** - same problem, don't have enough time

3) **open-minded - yes**, made friends with different people

4) (go) **went through - yes** - five boyfriends before husband

5) **down-to-earth - no** - Saturday afternoon music

6) (give it a shot) **give deep sea fishing a shot - no** - cancelled reservations

7) **get together - yes**, since last month - tomorrow

8) **blind date - yes** - look like, recognize each other

9) **in hot water - no** - A on test, finished homework early

10) (see) **seeing each other - yes** - spend every weekend together

11) (make) **made good time - yes** - arrived early

12) **hang on - yes** - 15 minutes before schedule appointment

13) **a sweet tooth - no** - chips, salsa

14) **a backseat driver - yes** - made me nervous

15) **get over - no** - five years for a toe

CHAPTER 5

Part I

Student 1 - p. 72

■ **Quick Fix**

1) 2

2) 4

3) 5

4) 3

5) 1

■ **Sense or Nonsense**

1) S

2) NS

3) S

4) S

5) NS

■ **Cloze It**

1) talked my ears off

2) a hunk

3) Long time, no see.

4) get along

5) comes in handy

■ **Plug In**

1) Long time, no see.

2) get along.

3) talks our ears off about football.

4) a hunk

5) comes in handy

Student 2 - p. 74

■ **Quick Fix**

1) 3

2) 4

3) 2

4) 1

5) 5

■ **Sense or Nonsense**

1) NS

2) S

3) NS

4) S

5) S

■ **Cloze It**

1) figure out

2) a morning person

3) has it together

4) rings a bell

5) come over

■ **Plug In**

1) is getting it together

2) figured out

3) This doesn't ring a bell

4) a morning person

5) come over

Student 3 - p. 76

■ **Quick Fix**

1) 2

2) 1

3) 5

4) 4

5) 3

■ **Sense or Nonsense**

1) NS

2) S

3) NS

4) NS

5) NS

■ **Cloze It**

1) a lemon

2) on my back

3) get in shape

4) broke up

5) pushy

■ **Plug In**

1) He's on my back

2) break up with him

3) pushy

4) a lemon

5) get in shape

Part II

Student 1 - p. 78

■ **Tell Me**

1) come in handy
2) talk someone's ears off
3) a hunk
4) get along
5) Long time no see

■ **Make This Make Sense (possible answers)**

1) Hunks DO usually make good models.
2) A good computer COMES in handy...
3) I LIKE to live with...
4) I saw you five YEARS ago...
5) I DON'T enjoy talking...

Student 2 - p. 79

■ **Tell Me**

1) ring a bell
2) have it together
3) come over
4) a night person
5) figure out

■ **Make This Make Sense (possible answers)**

1) ...after 3:00 P.M.
2) ...I REMEMBER...
3) It is really DIFFICULT...
4) NIGHT people...
5) ...She HAS it together...

Student 3 - p. 80

■ **Tell Me**

1) a lemon
2) break up
3) get in shape
4) pushy
5) on my back

■ **Make This Make Sense (possible answers)**

1) ....by NOT sitting...
2) ...is very HARD to do.
3) ...are NOT down-to-earth
4) ...are NOT lemons.
5) It's NOT easy...

Part III

CIRCLE AND DISCUSS - pp. 81-82

1) after 10:00 p.m., force myself to sleep (a night person)
2) how have you been doing, still with (long time no see)
3) give customers some space (pushy)
4) a headache, how much she can't stand talk my ears off)
5) after everything we ate (get in shape)
6) book plane, check out places, buy concert tickets, find out movies (come in handy)
7) as tall as (a hunk)
8) just don't remember (ring a bell)
9) beat each other up, growling (get along)
10) when school, work, study, have fun (figure out)
11) after school, look in fridge (come over
12) getting married, doesn't want to think about it (on someone's back)
13) cost more to fix than buy (a lemon)

14) long-term plans, pass TOEFL, met with advisor (get it together)
15) get back together, really love each other (break up)

FIND OUT - pp. 82-83

1)a) 2   b) 3   c) 1
2)a) Don't bug me about my hair
  b) stopped bugging me
3)a) bad physical condition, out of shape
  b) excellent physical condition
4) pushy (adjective), push (verb)
5)a) neat   b) handy, neat
6)a) 1, 3   b) 2   c) 2

Part IV

TUNE IN - p. 84

1) She **talked my ears off**...
2) It **didn't ring a bell**...
3) He was way too **pushy**...
4) It has definitely **come in handy**...
5) She really **has it together**...
6) He is **a hunk**...
7) I told him to **come over**...
8) he's **getting in shape**...
9) We seem to **get along**...
10) It didn't take very long for me to **figure out**...
11) It was **a lemon**...
12) I don't like to **be on his back**...
13) **Long time, no see**...
14) She's **a morning person**...
15) She had to **break up**...

CHAPTER 6

Part I

Student 1 - p. 88

■ **Quick Fix**

1) 5
2) 1
3) 4
4) 2
5) 3

■ **Cloze It**

1) easy come, easy go
2) know-it-all
3) neat
4) stressed out
5) has a crush on

■ **Sense or Nonsense**

1) S
2) S
3) NS
4) S
5) NS

■ **Plug In**

1) has a crush on her
2) neat
3) easy come, easy go
4) is a know-it-all
5) stressed out

- **Cloze It**
1) is into
2) a steal
3) ran into
4) shape up or ship out
5) fake

3) 2
4) 1
5) 4

- **Sense or Nonsense**
1) S
2) NS
3) S
4) S
5) S

- **Plug In**
1) shape up or ship out
2) a steal
3) fake
4) ran into
5) is into

Student 3 - p. 92
- **Quick Fix**
1) 4
2) 5
3) 2
4) 1
5) 3

- **Cloze It**
1) show up
2) stuck-up
3) folks
4) stuck with it
5) play the field

- **Sense or Nonsense**
1) NS
2) NS
3) S
4) NS
5) S

- **Plug In**
1) stick with it
2) folks
3) Playing the field
4) shows up
5) stuck-up

Part II

Student 1 - p. 94
- **Tell Me**
1) neat
2) a know-it-all
3) have a crush on someone
4) stressed out
5) easy come, easy go

- **Make This Make Sense (possible answers)**
1) I DON'T care VERY much...
2) ...because he is such a SWEETY.
3) Know-it-alls are NOT always...
4) Neat people make GOOD...
5) Being stressed out if BAD for...

Student 2 - p. 95
- **Tell Me**
1) run into
2) shape up or ship out
3) fake

- **Make This Make Sense (possible answers)**
1) It would be VERY surprising...
2) You SAVE SOME money...
3) I WOULD CARE...

4) be into
5) a steal

Student 3 - p. 96
- **Tell Me**
1) play the field
2) stuck-up
3) show up
4) folks
5) stick with it

4) ...you usually feel EXCITED.
5) YOU SHOULDN'T DO whatever...

- **Make This Make Sense (possible answers)**
1) You SHOULD stick ...
2) Stuck-up people USU-ALLY...
3) You SHOULDN'T play...
4) Teachers SOMETIMES...
5) It's NOT OK...

Part III

CIRCLE AND DISCUSS - pp. 97-98
1) can't give up, not going to quit, no pain, no gain (stick with it)
2) a crack-up, a hunk, nuts about (have a crush on)
3) three years ago, coincidence (run into)
4) mom, sister, brother (folks)
5) outspoken, tell me how to do my job, never worked in the field (a know-it-all)
6) follow the rules like everyone else (shape up or ship out)
7) take responsibility (easy come, easy go)
8) artificial, look real (fake)
9) go out with four women, busy guy (play the field)
10) saved over $300.00, sale, discount (a steal)
11) empty seats (show up)
12) love, like, dreamlike (neat)
13) take, develops, paints (be into)
14) call in sick, day off, kick back, relax, do as little as possible (stressed out)
15) complained, nothing was good enough (stuck-up)

FIND OUT - pp. 98-99
1)a) stressed me out (verb)
   b) was stressed out (adjective)
2)a) gerund   b) noun
3)a) 2, 2   b) 3, 1   c) 1, 3
4)a) 3   b) 1   c) 2
5)a) He's playing games...   b) ...a player!
6)a) The only person who ever washes the dishes.

Part IV

TUNE IN - p. 100
1) a know-it-all, statement, irritated
2) be into, question, happy
3) show up, question, neutral
4) neat, statement, happy

5) run into, question, happy
6) fake, question, irritated
7) folks, statement, neutral
8) have a crush on, question, happy
9) shape up or ship out, statement, irritated
10) stick with it, statement, neutral
11) stress out, statement, irritated
12) play the field, statement, neutral
13) a steal, question, happy
14) easy come, easy go, statement, neutral
15) stuck-up, question, irritated

CHAPTER 7

Part I

Student 1 -.p. 108

■ **Quick Fix**   ■ **Cloze It**

1) 2 **1)**   hit the sack
2) 5 **2)**   keep an eye on
3) 1 **3)**   a knockout
4) 3 **4)**   come up with
5) 4 **5)**   hot

■ **Sense or Nonsense**   ■ **Plug In**
1) S   1) hot
2) NS   2) the biggest knockouts
3) NS   3) come up with
4) NS   4) kept an eye on my neighbor's house.
5) NS   5) hit the sack

Student 2 -p. 110
■ **Quick Fix**   ■ **Cloze It**
1) 2   1) is nosy
2) 5   2) Back in a flash.
3) 1   3) take turns
4) 3   4) a chicken
5) 4   5) drop off

■ **Sense or Nonsense**   ■ **Plug In**
1) NS   1) nosy
2) NS   2) take turns
3) NS   3) chickens
4) S   4) be back in a flash!
5) NS   5) drop this off

Student 3 - p. 112
■ **Quick Fix**   ■ **Cloze It**
1) 4   1) step on it
2) 5   2) loaded
3) 2   3) put his foot in his

4) 1   mouth
5) 3   4) brains
     5) work out

■ **Sense or Nonsense**   ■ **Plug In**
1) NS   1) I put my foot in my mouth.
2) S   2) step on it
3) NS   3) worked out
4) NS   4) a brain
5) S   5) loaded

Part II

Student 1 - p. 114
■ **Tell Me**   ■ **Make This Make Sense (possible answers)**

1) come up with   1) ...I DON'T want to...
2) keep an eye on   2) You HAVE to...
3) a knockout   3) ...is hot, ALMOST EVERYONE...
4) hit the sack   4) Great teachers USUALLY...SOMETHING...
5) hot   5) ...covers ARE knockouts.

Student 2 - p. 115
■ **Tell Me**   ■ **Make This Make Sense (possible answers)**

1) drop off   1) ..it WOULDN'T take him...
2) back in a flash   2) ...makes a LOUSY...
3) take turns   3) ...drive-through is CONVENIENT.
4) nosy   4) A chicken WOULD be...
5) a chicken   5) It's VERY important...

Student 3 - p. 116
■ **Tell Me**   ■ **Make This Make Sense (possible answers)**

1) a brain   1) We DON'T have MUCH time...
2) loaded   2) ...work out DON'T usually...
3) put my foot in my mouth   3) Loaded people CAN...
4) step on it   4) ...WAS a brain.
5) work out   5) I CAN'T make...

Part III

CIRCLE AND DISCUSS - pp. 117-118
1) run to, about 20 minutes (back in a flash)
2) a great idea, really creative (come up with)

3) lots of energy, jogging, yoga (work out)

4) got home late, made it to morning class, beat (hit the sack)

5) curious, don't mean to, but do you mind (nosy)

6) First, looked great, then, get in shape (put one's foot in one's mouth)

7) be here for awhile, run to, don't want to carry (keep an eye on)

8) fell out, afraid to (a chicken)

9) get behind, already late, slowpoke (step on it)

10) gorgeous, look at her (a knockout)

11) pick up (drop off)

12) share fairly (take turns)

13) outstanding, scholarship (a brain)

14) in the world, popular (hot)

15) $300,000 every game, save income (loaded)

FIND OUT - pp. 118-119

1)a) 3   **b)** 1   **c)** 4   **d)** 2

2)a) drunk   **b)** full - ball players   **c)** full - bullets

3)a) brainy, brains

  b) She's the smartest, the boss, the mastermind

4)a) chickened out, chickens

5)a) knocked him out   **b)** knocks out

6)a) solve = separable, transitive, it = the problem

  b) exercising = intransitive   **c)** exercise = a noun

Part IV

TUNE IN - p. 120

1) hit the sack (past, statement)

2) a brain (present, question)

3) put my foot in my mouth (past, future, statement)

4) nosy (present, question)

5) drop me off (future, question)

6) a knockout (present, statement)

7) took turns (past, statement)

8) loaded (future, statement)

9) come up with (past, question)

10) back in a flash (present, statement)

11) kept an eye on (past statement)

12) step on it (present, question)

13) work out (present question)

14) a chicken (past, statement)

15) hot (question, future)

CHAPTER 8

Part I

Student 1 - p. 124

■ **Quick Fix**
1) 4
2) 5
3) 1
4) 2
5) 3

■ **Cloze It**
1) wild
2) turned down
3) shortcut
4) Let's call it a day.
5) lend her a hand

■ **Sense or Nonsense**
1) NS
2) S
3) S
4) NS
5) S

■ **Plug In**
1) lent a hand
2) shortcut
3) call it a night
4) wild
5) turn it down

Student 2 - p. 126

■ **Quick Fix**
1) 2
2) 5
3) 1
4) 3
5) 4

■ **Cloze It**
1) get even
2) lucked out
3) had time to kill
4) a bummer
5) fishing for compliments

■ **Sense or Nonsense**
1) S
2) S
3) NS
4) S
5) NS

■ **Plug In**
1) had time to kill
2) a bummer
3) fishing for compliments
4) lucked out
5) get even with you

Student 3 - p. 128

■ **Quick Fix**
1) 4
2) 3
3) 1
4) 5
5) 2

■ **Cloze It**
1) tough
2) climbing the walls
3) straighten it up
4) get it
5) sixth sense

■ **Sense or Nonsense**
1) S
2) S
3) NS
4) S
5) NS

■ **Plug In**
1) straightens up
2) tough
3) climbing the walls
4) get it
5) sixth sense

Part II

Student 1 - p. 130

■ Tell Me	■ Make This Make Sense (possible answers)
1) wild	1) ...has made some very wild music videos.
2) turn down	2) ...you SHOULD...
3) a shortcut	3) ...you SHOULD...
4) call it a day/night	4) Shortcuts DON'T make...
5) lend a hand	5) TURN down a...

Student 2 - p. 131

■ Tell Me	■ Make This Make Sense (possible answers)
1) a bummer	1) ...is ON your back...
2) have time to kill	2) OPEN-minded...
3) luck out	3) ...probably DON'T fish...
4) fish for compliments	4) I DON'T have to...
5) get even	5) ...you DON'T have an...

Student 3 - p. 132

■ Tell Me	■ Make This Make Sense (possible answers)
1) climb the walls	1) ...are EASY to...
2) get it	2) You are NOT going to...
3) sixth sense	3) You SHOULD...
4) straighten up	4) I DON'T look forward to...
5) tough	5) ...it looks NEAT.

Part III

CIRCLE AND DISCUSS - pp. 133-134
1) beat, five times, poor sport (get even)
2) truck, help moving (lend a hand)
3) little voice inside, usually right (sixth sense)
4) didn't get to take, disappointed (a bummer)
5) make great time, new freeway open (shortcut)
6) keep cat inside (climb the walls)
7) so happy, done so well, doesn't care (fish for compliments)
8) wasn't sure how long (turn down)
9) so much stuff, couldn't park car (straighten up)
10) climbing the Athabasca Glacier...magnificent British Columbia (the wildest)
11) normally too busy (have time to kill)
12) carpets washed, spilled coffee again (get it)
13) happy hour, dinner, movie, dancing, coffee (call it a night)
14) great parking place, rain, stuff to carry (luck out)
15) complex writing system, differences male/female speech (tough)

FIND OUT - pp. 134-135
1) a) off   b) down   c) up   d) on
2) a) make behave   b) clear up
3) a) understand   b) bought
4) a) are even   b) Is it even
5) a) bums me out (verb), a bummer (noun), bummed out (adjective)

Part IV

TUNE IN - p.136
1) flattery - fish for compliments - irritated
2) pitch in - lend a hand - happy
3) your time will come - get even - irritated
4) tidy - straighten up - neutral
5) decline - turn down - neutral
6) deja-vu - sixth sense - happy
7) a shame - a bummer - irritated
8) fantastic - wild - happy
9) challenges - tough - neutral
10) turn in - call it a night - happy
11) go nuts - climb the walls - irritated
12) do nothing - have time to kill - happy
13) scolded - get it - irritated
14) hit the jackpot - luck out - happy
15) the way to go - a shortcut - neutral

CHAPTER 9

Part I

Student 1 - p. 140

■ Quick Fix	■ Cloze It
1) 4	1) Better late than never.
2) 3	2) weird
3) 5	3) has had it
4) 1	4) the works
5) 2	5) count on

■ Sense or Nonsense	■ Plug In
1) S	1) has had it
2) S	2) Better late than never.
3) NS	3) weird
4) NS	4) the works
5) S	5) You can count on me.

Student 2 - p. 142

■ **Quick Fix**
1) 3
2) 1
3) 4
4) 5
5) 2

■ **Cloze It**
1) a sweetheart
2) fed up with
3) wishy-washy
4) out in left field
5) turned in

■ **Sense or Nonsense**
1) NS
2) S
3) NS
4) S
5) S

■ **Plug In**
1) turn this letter in
2) am fed up with
3) a sweetheart
4) is out in left field
5) be wishy-washy

Student 3 - p. 144

■ **Quick Fix**
1) 3
2) 1
3) 2
4) 5
5) 4

■ **Cloze It**
1) for real
2) creepy
3) fill in
4) have it wired
5) a blast

■ **Sense or Nonsense**
1) NS
2) S
3) S
4) NS
5) S

■ **Plug In**
1) a blast
2) creepy
3) for real
4) he has it wired
5) fill me in on

Part II

Student 1 - p. 146

■ **Tell Me**
1) weird
2) the works
3) have had it
4) count on

5) better late than never

■ **Make This Make Sense (possible answers)**
1) It's EASY to...
2) You're GOING TO...
3) ...sound BAD...
4) ...so GIVE me SOME pickles AND
5) ...FELT weird...

Student 2 - p. 147

■ **Tell Me**
1) wishy-washy
2) fed up with
3) a sweetheart
4) turn in
5) out in left field

■ **Make This Make Sense (possible answers)**
1) ...are BAD employees
2) ...I DON'T keep it...
3) ...you DON'T want to...
4) It's HARD to...
5) It's NOT difficult...

Student 3 - p. 148

■ **Tell Me**
1) creepy
2) a blast

3) have it wired
4) for real

5) fill in

■ **Make This Make Sense (possible answers)**
1) ...usually HAVE TO...
2) It's NOT a blast...It's a bummer
3) ...it's EASY for...
4) Creepy movies AREN'T...
5) You SHOULD trust...

Part III

CIRCLE AND DISCUSS - pp. 149-150
1) sausage, pepperoni, ham, olives, onions, peppers, mushrooms, cheese (the works)
2) bizarre, middle of the night (creepy)
3) bring me over chicken soup, my favorite magazines (a sweetheart)
4) made lots of new friends, visited SF and LA, body boarding, learned English (a blast)
5) doesn't listen, everyone, keeps quitting (out in left field)
6) too soft, sinks in middle, get a new one (have had it)
7) requests for vacation, by the end of the month (turn in)
8) Dad is a mechanic, grew up, repair cars (have something wired)
9) always give you good advice, very fair, use sixth sense (count on)
10) the truth (for real)
11) the day after (better late than never)
12) can't decide, good, but might be better (wishy-washy)
13) just saw...but now don't know where it is (weird)
14) overworked, underpaid (fed up with)
15) form, carefully, mistakes (fill in)

FIND OUT - pp. 150-151
1) a) 3   b) 1   c) 2
2) a) out   b) in   c) in
3) a) fed up with   b) worn out
4) a) face the truth   b) absolute
5) a) OK   e) OK   h) OK
6) a) creepy, gives me the creeps
7) a) 2   b) 3   c) 1

Part IV

1) the works
2) wishy-washy
3) for real
4) count on
5) turn in
6) creepy
7) have had it
8) a sweetheart
9) a blast
10) better late than never
11) fill in
12) weird
13) fed up with
14) have something wired
15) out in left field

Review: Chapters 1-2-3

Dialogue Match, p. 51
Partner A: 1, 9, 5, 3, 11, 7   **Partner B:** 8, 2, 12, 4, 10, 6

Shout It Out, p. 52 (possible answers)
Student 2

1) give up
4) goof off
2) go blank
5) money to burn
3) cool
6) be broke

Student 3

1) If you want to give up smoking, you'd better get with it!
2) You should practice more so that you don't go blank.
3) That sounds like a really cool place to work.
4) It's fun to goof off at work sometimes.
5) Since you have some money to burn, I'll be your buddy!
6) It's hard to be broke all the time. Why don't you get another job?

Review: Chapters 4-5-6

Dialogue Match, p. 104
Partner A: 9, 1, 11, 7, 3, 5   **Partner B:** 4, 6, 2, 10, 8, 12

The Great Egghead Race, p. 105

1) shape up or ship out
2) a morning person
3) come in handy
4) a steal
5) play games

Review: Chapters 7-8-9

Dialogue Match, p. 156   p. 157
Partner A: 5, 9, 3, 1, 11, 7   **Partner B:** 8, 4, 2, 12, 6, 10

Answer Key   **173**

TRANSCRIPTS: TUNE IN

Chapter 1, pg. 15 (key words are <u>underlined</u>)

1) We had the most <u>fabulous</u> French food last weekend. It was beautifully presented and so delicious! (awesome)
2) We really hope that you'll be able to buy that gorgeous house. You have our <u>best wishes</u>! (keep our fingers crossed)
3) I'm <u>in the mood for</u> inviting some friends over to hang out and play cards. (feel like)
4) We need to get more information to <u>evaluate</u> whether or not this is the best price for our education. (check out)
5) Linda is a great <u>pal</u> of mine. We met each other at work eight years ago. (buddy)
6) That movie was so stupid, but I <u>laughed till I cried</u>! (crack up)
7) It's interesting to <u>socialize</u> with people from different countries. (hang out)
8) Daniel is <u>crazy about</u> Sabine. He's always inviting her to do something. (nuts about)
9) Scott is the biggest <u>idiot</u> I've ever met. All he thinks about is himself. (a jerk)
10) Karl is going to make lots of <u>cash</u> in his new business because it is doing so well. (bucks)
11) If we want to see that show, we've got to <u>eat fast</u> or we'll miss the beginning. (grab a bite)
12) Look, I was just <u>joking</u>. Don't be so serious. (kidding)
13) <u>Don't worry</u> about finishing this today. We'll have more time next week. (no big deal)
14) James <u>can't buy</u> anything new for a while because he just got a new Jeep. (be broke)
15) Your new computer is really <u>neat</u>! I love the subwoofer speaker too! (cool)

Chapter 2, pg. 30

1) Even though <u>giving up</u> smoking is really hard, you should do it because it's better for your health. (yes)
2) A lot of people think that Sharon Stone is a <u>show-off</u> because of some of her earlier movies. (yes)
3) I feel like <u>kicking back</u> this weekend, so let's paint the house, plant a new garden, and work on the cars. (no)
4) Kate takes care of her boys and husband, works full-time, and serves on several committees. At the end of the day, she never <u>feels beat</u>. (no)
5) Mel Gibson is <u>a big nerd</u> because he's an actor, director and producer as well as a husband and father of six children. (no)
6) Mark McGuire, who has hit more home runs than anyone in the world, definitely has a <u>no pain, no gain</u> attitude. That's why he is a baseball legend! (yes)
7) Oh, <u>never mind</u>, don't worry about forgetting your homework and being late again and again. I'm sure you'll get a good grade. (no)
8) Mike Tyson <u>is</u> so <u>classy</u> and such a good sport that he never seems to get in trouble with the law! (no)
9) Nothing <u>bugs</u> me more than eating delicious food and drinking fine wine with good friends. (no)
10) Bill was so embarrassed because he forgot my name on our first date. He <u>went</u> completely <u>blank</u>. (yes)
11) Pierre usually plays ice hockey twice a month. That's the only sport he does, so I don't think he's <u>a jock</u>. (yes)
12) Rie and Matthew are very friendly and <u>laid-back</u>. That's why they have so many friends. (yes)
13) I <u>can't stand</u> people who never seem to have enough money when you go out. They borrow $5.00 here, $10.00 there and never remember to pay you back. (yes)
14) Roxanne <u>fell for Ahmed</u> because he is such a funny, kind, smart, and generous man. (yes)
15) My brother had <u>money to burn</u> because he won $500 in Las Vegas playing craps. (yes)

Chapter 3, pg. 45 (key words are in *italics*)

1) Stefan thinks he is more *important than* other people. He does exactly what he wants to do and he doesn't care if he keeps you waiting. Don't waste your time with him! (a big head)
2) We've got until 4:30 maximum to finish this and mail it. The post office closes at 5:30! We'd better *concentrate* and *work hard*! (get with it)
3) I don't *really feel like working* right now. I think I'll take a break and play with the computer a little. (goof off/around)
4) I can't believe I bought this coat! I *thought it was real* leather! I spent almost 300 bucks on it! They cheated me! (rip off)
5) I'm *so busy* this week I won't be able to do anything but work. Next week will be better. (swamped)

6) I really wish you would *learn to clean up* after yourself! I'm tired of being the only person who does the dishes or takes out the trash! (a slob)

7) Let's put on our *hot clothes*, go downtown for some Italian food, and then go dancing. (dressed to kill)

8) I *lost my temper* with my boyfriend and screamed at him. Now he won't talk to me! I think I made a *mistake*! (blow it)

9) You *had better* stop playing your music so loud in the morning, or all the neighbors are going to be mad at you! (cut it out)

10) We *have to do some research* for our project. Let's go *study* at the library. (hit the books)

11) Don't give me that *stupid* excuse! What you did *wasn't fair* at all! (bogus)

12) Oh, *I see. I can guess* why you didn't go out with him again. He probably kept you waiting all afternoon! (I bet)

13) Don't *tease* him if he's not as bright as you are! Don't *criticize*! Grow up! Act your age, not your shoe size! (put down)

14) Sorry, I don't want to *go out with* anyone for awhile, so don't try to *arrange* anything for me. I've had enough jerks! (fix someone up)

15) I just love those salt and pepper *potato chips*! I could eat the whole bag! (junk food)

Chapter 4, pg. 64

1) I'm **looking forward to** studying all weekend long because I have three tests on Monday. (no - studying all weekend, three tests)

2) Carlos and I have the same problem. We don't have enough time to finish our work. We're **in the same boat**. (yes - same problem, don't have enough time...)

3) Yoko has made friends with a lot of people from different countries because she is so **open-minded**. (yes, made friends with different people...)

4) Sabine knows what she wants and needs in a relationship because she **went through** five boyfriends before she met her husband. (yes - five boyfriends)

5) My neighbor is so **down-to-earth** because he always complains that we play our music too loudly, even on Saturday afternoon. (no - Saturday afternoon music...)

6) We decided to **give deep sea diving a shot**, so we cancelled our reservations to go. (no - canceled reservations...)

7) Kim and I **get together** at least once a month for coffee. We haven't seen each other since last month, and today is our day to get together. (yes, since last month, today)

8) We had to tell each other what we looked like so we

would recognize each other at the restaurant when we went on our **blind date**. (yes - look like, recognize each other)

9) Enrique is **in hot water** again! He got another A on his test, and he finished his homework early. (no - A on test, finished homework early...)

10) Nick and Mary started **seeing each other** about four months ago and now they spend every weekend together. (yes - spend every weekend together...)

11) We **made good time** coming home. Our plane arrived early because of going in the same direction as the wind. (yes - arrived early)

12) I called the dentist, but I had to **hang on** the phone for almost 15 minutes before I could schedule an appointment. (yes - 15 minutes before scheduling appointment...)

13) Georgia asked me to go to the store to get her some chips and salsa because she has such a **sweet tooth**. (no - chips, salsa...)

14) The taxi driver in New York City made me so nervous by the way he drove that I felt like **a backseat driver**. (yes - made me nervous...)

15) Deborah broke her toe, and it took her about five years to **get over it**. (no - five years for a toe...)

Chapter 5, pg. 79

1) Beginning: Sally kept going on and on and on about how much she couldn't stand the management decisions. She
End: (talked my ears off) for two hours about how many mistakes they made!

2) Beginning: We just couldn't remember exactly what they had told us to do,
End: because it (didn't ring a bell) at first, but finally something was familiar.

3) Beginning: That man was really annoying. He was drunk, and he was way too
End: (pushy) when he kept asking us to dance even though we had told him no.

4) Beginning: My cellular phone is great! It has definitely
End: (come in handy) because I can use it whenever I need to.

5) Beginning: Maria just finished studying engineering and she has started work, but she is going to continue studying. I think she
End: really (has it together) because she always has plans to improve herself.

6) Beginning: John was a really skinny boy, but he filled out more and more and now he
End: is (a hunk)! All the girls at school seem to like him.

7) Beginning: James gets home from work at six and

then works out at the gym, so I told him to
End: (come over) to our place at eight-thirty.

8) Beginning: For the past month, Harrison has been exercising, taking vitamins, and eating organic food, so he is
End: (getting in shape). He says he feels great and has a lot of energy.

9) Beginning: I really like my neighbors Margie and Sonny. They're always so friendly and helpful. We seem to
End: (get along) well. If I need anything, I know I can ask them.

10) Beginning: It didn't take me very long to
End: (figure out) how to input the phone numbers in my new telephone.

11) Beginning: The car that we leased always had so many problems. It was
End: (a lemon). I'm glad we could trade it in for a new one!

12) Beginning: I'm really tired of my roommate being such a slob, but I don't like to
End: (be on his back) about how messy he is all the time.

13) Beginning: I can't believe it's you!
End: (Long time, no see) You haven't changed at all!

14) Beginning: Stephanie loves to get up really early before anyone else because she is
End: (a morning person). By the time everyone else gets up, she has already started her day.

15) Beginning: He refused to listen to her, so she had to
End: (break up) with him because there was no compromise.

Chapter 6, pg. 94

1) Ugh! Dan never listens to anyone because he thinks he's smarter than everyone else! He is the biggest **know-it-all** I've ever met! (statement, irritated)

2) **I'm into** windsurfing these days! It is so much fun. I take lessons at Mission Bay. Have you ever gotten into a water sport? (question, happy)

3) I think we'll probably start everything around eight-thirty or nine. What time do you think most people will **show up**? (question, neutral)

4) Oh, your new job sounds so **neat**! Congratulations. Now you won't only make more money, but you'll also be doing something you really enjoy! (statement, happy)

5) You'll never guess who I ran into yesterday! Kelly Harris! I'm surprised we recognized each other! Can you believe we ran into each other? It's been years! (question, happy)

6) Ugh, not another Terry story! What did she do

now? Was she showing off her new BMW? Can you believe how **fake** she is? (question, irritated)

7) I usually see my **folks** once a month. They live in Los Angeles. It takes about two hours to get to their house. (statement, neutral)

8) Oh, my! Sean has been so friendly lately. Is it my imagination, or do you think he **has a little crush on** me? (question, happy)

9) You have really got to get serious Kazu! You'd better get with it or you'll fail! It's high time to **shape up or ship out**! (statement, irritated)

10) Learning English is really frustrating right now, and the quarter is almost over, but I'm going to keep hitting the books and **stick with it**! (statement, neutral)

11) Oh no, not another test! I already have tests on Monday, Tuesday and Wednesday! AND our final exam is on Thursday! I'm so **stressed out**! (statement, irritated)

12) Anna told me she wanted to go out with me, but she also seems interested in going out with other guys too. I think she's **playing the field** right now. (statement, neutral)

13) You bought this big new television for only a hundred and fifty dollars. What **a steal**! I want one too! Where did you find that? (question, happy)

14) Michael moved to Las Vegas, got a great new job and bought a new house. He only gambles with two hundred dollars a month because he knows it's **easy come, easy go**. (statement, neutral)

15) Those girls are beautiful, but they have zero personality! They wouldn't even talk to us once they found out that we're students. Can you believe how **stuck-up** they are? (question, irritated)

Chapter 7, pg. 112

1) I'm going to **hit the sack** early tonight because I have to get up really early tomorrow. (future, statement)

2) Mayumi seems really smart. She always knows the answers. She's **a brain**, isn't she? (present, question) I can't believe what I said yesterday. I felt so embarrassed. I don't want to ever **put my foot in my mouth** again. (past, future, statement)

3) What do you think of Gloria? Does she ask you as many personal questions as she asks me? Doesn't she seem a bit **nosy**? (present, question)

5) I have a big test tomorrow, and I need to study a lot. Could you **drop me off** at school a little earlier tomorrow? (future, question)

6) So many people think that Demi Moore is **a knock-out**, but I think she's really fake. (present, statement)

7) We went to the desert yesterday afternoon and **took turns** driving Michael's new Jeep. (past, statement)

8) If Max keeps on investing his money so well, he's going to be **loaded** some day soon. (future, statement)

9) How did you **come up with** such a great way to fix this computer bug?? (past, question)

10) Go ahead and begin without me. I'll be **back in a flash**. (present/future, statement)

11) Diane **kept an eye on** my house and took care of my dog while I was in New York. (past, statement)

12) Hey, aren't we going to be late? Don't you think you should **step on it**? (present, question)

13) How do you stay in such great shape? How often do you **work out**? (present, question)

14) It's hard to believe that "Jim the jock" used to be such **a chicken** about doing any kind of sport. (past, statement)

15) Who do you think will become the **hot** new Hollywood star next year? (question, future)

Chapter 8, page 127 (key words in *italics*)

1) Samantha is always looking for *flattery* about how good she looks. (fish for compliments - irritated)

2) Everyone *pitched in* and we got the office completely set up really fast. (lend a hand - happy)

3) Glen was so angry after he lost that he told me, "*Your time will come* and I'll win." (get even - irritated)

4) Your desk is so neat and *tidy*. When did you have time to clean it? (straighten up - neutral)

5) He had to *decline* their job offer because he didn't want to move his family again. (turn down - neutral)

6) I've seen you somewhere before. I'm having *deja-vu*. (sixth sense - happy)

7) That is such a *shame* that you and your girlfriend broke up. You were such a cute couple. (a bummer - irritated, upset)

8) We had a *fantastic* time when we went skiing in France and Switzerland last year. It was so exciting! (wild - happy)

9) Getting a good job is one of the biggest *challenges* people have to face. (tough – neutral)

10) It's two-thirty in the morning. I had a great time, but it's time to *turn in*. (call it a night - happy)

11) Everyone *is going nuts* with all the noise from the construction! (climb the walls - irritated)

12) Sometimes it's great to *do nothing*. (have time to kill - happy)

13) The policeman *scolded* me for driving too fast, and he gave me a ticket. (get it - irritated, upset)

14) If I choose number 7, I often *hit the jackpot*. (luck out - happy)

15) This is *the way to go*. You miss most of the traffic. (a shortcut - neutral)

Chapter 9, page 142

1) How do you like your pizzas, hamburgers, or sandwiches? (the works)

2) When was the last time it was difficult for you to make a decision? (wishy-washy)

3) Describe a sincere and genuine person you know. (for real)

4) Who is a person you can depend on? How? (count on)

5) Are you good at submitting your homework when it is due? (turn in)

6) What is one of the scariest places you have ever seen? (creepy)

7) Do you have a pair of jeans or shoes you love but that are almost dead? (have had it)

8) Who is a person that you like a lot because they are so thoughtful? (a sweetheart)

9) What is something that you love to do because it's so much fun? (a blast)

10) What is something that you feel is not too late to try? (better late than never)

11) When you miss class, who lets you know what happened? (fill in)

12) What is one of the strangest things you have seen or heard? (weird)

13) What do you do when you can't tolerate doing something anymore? (fed up with)

14) What is something you know how to do easily and naturally? (have something wired)

15) Describe someone whose opinions you think are very mistaken. (out in left field)

SUGGESTION BOX

More Ways to Practice Using the Expressions

■ **Games**

1. **Tic-Tac-Toe:** Create your own game.

2. **Bingo:** - Make a grid of 25 squares. Choose 25 expressions and ask your classmates to write them in the grid. Then describe the expressions. The first person to get 5 in a row is the winner.

3. **Password:** On index cards, write expressions of your choice to practice describing to your partner.

4. **Hot Seat:** In groups of 3 or 4, one person is seated on the "hot seat" and cannot see the board. The teacher writes an expression on the board for the students to describe to the person on the hot seat. As soon as the person knows the expression, he or she jumps up and shouts it out. The first group to get the expression wins a point.

5. **Hangman:** Practice spelling by playing this game.

6. **The Great Race:** Students form teams of 4 or 5. One student or the teacher randomly chooses expressions to describe. Whichever team writes the expression on the board the fastest wins.

7. **Jeopardy:** Arrange the expressions into categories. For example: Expressions that have two meanings (turn down, get it, work out...), Expressions which can change grammatical categories (nerd - nerdy, crack up - a crack up, bum someone out - bummed out...), Expressions which may be said in an annoyed tone (a lemon, put down, a jerk...). One student can be the host and ask, "For 5 points, What is a crack up? The student contestant may answer, "It's a noun which can also be a phrasal verb. Extra points can be given for sentences using the target expression.

8. **Mime:** Select expressions which lend themselves to being mimed: talk someone's ears off, be beat, crack up, down-to-earth, a backseat driver...

9. **Whispers:** One student writes a sentence using target expressions and then says it to the next student who repeats it around the room until the final student hears it.

10. **Basketball:** Divide the class into two teams. Select 3 point expressions and 2 point expressions. Fouls given for wrong definitions, inability to define, speaking out of turn. Free throws will be given for any foul.

11. **Baseball:** On the board, draw a baseball diamond and use adhesive notes

with team names on them. Select expressions for single, double, and home run questions. Each team member gets one chance to define or spell correctly. Any error is a strike. Three strikes and you're out.

12. Big Bucks Pyramid: On index cards, write expressions which have synonyms or antonyms. Put the cards face down. One student selects the card and reads the expression to the other student, who must come up with either a synonym or antonym. Encourage the students to go as fast as possible. Whichever team gets through the most cards goes to the top of the pyramid.

13. Go Fish: In pairs, students draw one expression, write a two-line dialogue within 2 minutes and perform it to the class.

14. Chain Story: One student begins a story using a target expression in a sentence. The next student continues the story by writing another sentence, and so on. The group of students who writes a story using the greatest number of expressions wins.

15. List It: In a limited time, students write down as many expressions as they can remember.

■ REVIEWS: GRAND FINALE OPTIONS

Students select their favorite Grand Finale dialogue or story. Selections can be put into a classbook so that everyone can read them. Students may also perform their dialogues or read their stories to the whole class. This is a great pronunciation activity.

■ NEW EXPRESSIONS: CHAPTER CREATION

As a final project, put the students into groups of 2 or 3 to create their own chapter using some of the expressions they have brought to class in their Expression Logs. The students can model their chapter after those in the book. The teacher can also require that certain components be included in the chapters that the students create. For example:

Definitions and Examples, Quick Fix, Cloze It, Sense or Nonsense, Make this Make Sense, Circle and Discuss, and Tune In, or The Chat Room.

Students can share their chapters with their classmates. They can also make textbook of all their chapters.

■ BINGO

		Bingo		

■ JEOPARDY - Use adhesive notes to cover the boxes with the target expressions.

Points	Expresssions that	Expresssions that	Expresssions that	Expresssions that
5				
10				
15				
20				

1. GRAMMATICAL CATEGORIES

In English, you can increase your vocabulary by changing a word into another grammatical category. For example, a nerd is classified as a noun, but it may also become an adjective, nerdy. It's important to notice the order of words. For example, articles such as "a" or "the" are followed by nouns, verbs like "be" or "seem" frequently precede adjectives, and adjectives go before nouns:

"Bill **is** **the** **nerdiest** **nerd**."
verb   article   adjective   noun

It's also important to notice word endings such as –ed, which may be the regular simple past tense or it may indicate a participle adjective. Did you know that many verbs can be made into adjectives by putting them into their present or past participle form? Yes, that's right! Verbs that become adjectives in this manner are called participle adjectives. For example, **stress out** is a phrasal verb, but **stressed out** is an adjective formed from the past participle of the verb as in

"I'm **stressed out** because too much homework **stresses me out**."
participle adjective   phrasal verb

Below is a grid of the expressions in this book which may change grammatical categories.

Expression	Noun	Verb	Adjective	Adverb
beat		It beats me.	be beat.	
brain	a brain/the brains		brainy	
break up	a break-up	break up		
bummer	a bummer	bum someone out	be bummed out	
bug	a bug	bug someone		
chicken	a chicken	chicken out		
crack up	a crack up	crack up		
creepy	a creep/the creeps	creep someone out	creepy	
drag	a drag	drag		
fill in	a fill-in			
a fox			foxy	
a freak			freaky	
knockout	a knockout	knock out		
loaded	a load	load	loaded	
nerd	a nerd		nerdy	

Expression	Noun	Verb	Adjective	Adverb
nuts	a nut		nutty/be nuts	nuts about
pick up	a pick up	pick up		
pushy	a push	push	pushy	
put down	a put-down	put down		
steal	a steal	steal		
stress out		stress someone out	be stressed out	
turn off	a turn off	turn off	be turned off	
turn on	a turn on	turn on	be turned on	
turn out	a turn out	turn out		
work out	a workout	work out		

2. PHRASAL VERBS

In English, phrasal verbs can be separable or inseparable. If they are separable, they have an object, which means they are transitive. If they are inseparable, they do not have an object and are intransitive. Sometimes a phrasal verb can be transitive or intransitive, but the meaning changes. For example, when the phrasal verb check out is separable, it has an object and it means to get information about something or someone. When it is intransitive, it means to leave a hotel.

Separable phrasal verbs have a special rule. When the object is in the pronoun form, the phrasal verb must be separated: **Let's** check out **that new store = Let's** check **it** out.

The object is that new store, and the corresponding pronoun is it. You could also say **Let's** check **that new store** out. But generally, if the object consists of more than four words, you shouldn't separate the phrasal verb. For example: **Let's** check **that new store by the beach** out. This sounds strange because there are too many words between the phrasal verb. It's better to say **Let's** check out **that new store by the beach**.

Below is a table of the phrasal verbs in this book:

Phrasal Verb	Separable	Inseparable
blow up	X - enlarge, explode	X - get angry
break down	X - understand, take apart	X - stop functioning
break out	X - open	X - begin, erupt
break up	X - stop, take apart	X - end a relationship
bum someone out	X	
check out	X - get information	X - leave a hotel
chicken out		X

Phrasal Verb	Separable	Inseparable
clean up	X - make clean, improve	
come on		X
come over		X
come up with		X
count on		X
crack up	X - make laugh	X - laugh, go crazy
drop off	X	
fall for		X
fed up with		X
figure out	X	
fill in	X - complete, inform	X - substitute
fill out	X - complete	X - grow
find out	X	
fix up	X	
get along		X
get over		X
give up	X	
go out with		X
go through		X
goof off/around		X
grow up		X
hang around		X
hang on		X
help out	X	
hold on		X
kick back		X
knock out	X	
look for		X
look forward to		X
luck out		X
pick up	X	
pitch in		X
pop in	X - put something somewhere	X - visit unexpectedly
put down	X - criticize, lay something down	

Phrasal Verb	Separable	Inseparable
put up with		X
rip off	X	
run into		X
run out of		X
set up	X	
settle for		X
show off	X	
show up		X
stick with		X
straighten out	X	
straighten up	X	
stress out	X	
take charge of		X
turn down	X	
turn in	X	
turn off	X	
turn on	X	
turn out	X	
turn up	X - increase volume	X - appear
wear out	X	
work out	X - solve	X - exercise

3. GERUNDS

Gerunds have the same form as the present participle of verbs, but they act like nouns. Think of gerunds as verb-nouns. In English, many idiomatic expressions with a preposition are followed by gerunds, and these expressions just need to be memorized. The chart below contains all the expressions in this book that must be followed by a gerund or noun.

Expression	Gerund - example	Noun/Pronoun - example
be into	swimming	sports
bummed out about	smoking	him
can't stand	shopping	jerks
check out	surfing	the city
chicken out of	skiing	school

Expression	Gerund - example	Noun/Pronoun - example
fed up with	cleaning	chores
feel like	eating	chocolate
find out about	studying	the movie
get stuck with	driving	the mess
give up	smoking	coffee
help out	taking care of	Lisa
look forward to	sleeping	vacation
be nuts about	cycling	dogs
settle for	staying	less money
show off	singing	the kids
stick with	working	school
take charge of	supervising	the employees
turn down	going	the promotion

INDEX - GLOSSARY

Expression	Chapter	Page	Meaning
get rich quick**VP	3	46	not a trustworthy way to make money
get rid of**:VP	5	77	throw away, trash
get stuck with*: VP	6	99	carry the responsibility
get stuck**: VP	1, 2	2, 21	not be able to move
get to know**: VP	4	58	become familiar
get to*: VP, PV	3	47	able to
get together: VP	4	58	spend time with, hang out, socialize
get with it: VP	3	36	become busy, focused, SL
give/have/take a shot*: VP	4	60	try, attempt
give someone the creeps*: VP	9	151	make someone feel weird, scared
give someone space**:VP	5	82	give someone some time or solitude
give up: PV	2	20	stop, quit
go blank: VP	2	22	suddenly forget
go for it**: VP	4	60	give it a shot, try
go nuts**: VP	8	136	feel crazy
go out with: PV	2	23	spend time together
go through: PV	4	60	experience, finish, use up
goof around/off: PV	3	38	play, fool around
grab a bite: VP	1	2	eat quickly
grow up**: PV	9	150	mature
gut feeling**:NP	8	129	intuition, sixth sense
handy*: ADJP	5	83	convenient, useful
hang around**: PV	8	127	spend time somewhere
hang in there*: VP	4	67	don't give up, don't quit, stick with it
hang on: PV	4	58	wait, don't give up
hang out: PV	1	6	spend time, socialize
happy hour**: NP	8	134	time of reduced drink prices
have a crush on: VP	6	88	like someone a lot
have had it: VP	9	140	worn out, fed up with
have/get it together: VP	5	74	be organized, have direction
have something wired: VP	9	144	know how to do something very well, SL
have time to kill: VP	8	126	have extra time
help out**: PV	5	75	assist, pitch in, lend a hand
high time**: NP	5	82	do it now, it's almost too late, SL
hit the books: VP	3	40	study
hit the road**: VP	8	126	leave
hit the sack: VP	7	108	go to bed
hold something against someone**: VP	8	127	keep bad feelings, not forgive
hold on*: PV	4	67	wait
honey*: NP	9	151	sweetheart, dear
hot: ADJP	7	108	popular, spicy, sexy, stolen, winning, SL
hunch**:NP	8	128	gut feeling, intuition, suspicion
hunk, a: NP	5	72	good-looking man, SL
I bet: P	3	36	I understand
in for it**	4	59	get in trouble soon, in hot water, SL
in great shape*: ADVP	5	83	be in excellent physical condition
in hot water: ADVP	4	58	be in trouble, be in for it
in the same boat: ADVP	4	56	have the same experience
into, be: VP	6	90	be very interested in something
jerk: NP	1	4	rude person, SL
jock, a: NP	2	20	person who does a lot of sports, SL
junk food: NP	3	38	food that isn't nutritious, SL
junk mail*: NP	3	47	worthless mail, SL

Expression	Chapter	Page	Meaning
punch it**: VP	7	113	drive faster, step on it
puppy love**: NP	6	88	young love
push*: VP	5	83	be aggressive, try to convince
pushy: ADJP	5	76	aggressive, bullying
put down: PV	3	40	criticize
put one's foot in			
one's mouth: VP	7	112	unintentionally say something wrong/insensitive
put up with**: PV	9	143	tolerate
ring a bell: VP	5	74	remember, recall
rip off: PV	3	36	steal, cheat, SL
run into: PV	6	90	meet by chance
run out of*:PV	6	99	finish, use up, go through
run*: VP	6	99	leave
rush hour**: NP	1	3	busy traffic
second nature**: NP	9	145	very natural for someone
see someone: VP	4	58	date, have an appointment with
see*: VP	4	66	understand, vision
set up**: PV	5	74	arrange, organize
settle for**: PV	4	66	accept
shape up or ship out: VP	6	90	follow the rules or leave
shortcut, a: NP	8	124	a quicker way
show off: PV	2	22	get attention
show up: PV	6	92	appear, come, find
six-pack**: NP	7	119	six beers
sixth sense: NP	8	128	intuition
slob, a: NP	3	36	messy, unclean person, SL
slowpoke**: NP	7	118	person who is slow
sooner or later**: ADVP	8	127	eventually
spaced out**: ADJP	R	158	feel tired, unable to concentrate, SL
state-of-the-art**: ADJP	7	113	the most current, modern
steal, a: NP	6	90	bargain, SL
step on it: VP	7	112	drive faster, hurry up, punch it
stick it out*: VP	6	99	endure, don't give up, stick with it
stick with: PV	6	92	don't give up, tolerate, finish, keep at it
straighten out*: PV	8	135	resolve, behave better
straighten up: PV	8	128	clean up, tidy, behave, solve
stress out: PV	6	88	make feel pressure, tension
stressed out*: ADJP	6	98	feel pressure, tension
stuck-up: ADJP	6	92	conceited, big ego, feel superior
stud*: NP	5	83	strong, tough man, SL
Sunday driver*: NP	4	67	person who drives slowly
swamped, be: ADJP	3	38	too busy
sweet tooth, a: NP	4	58	like to eat sugar
sweetheart, a: NP	9	142	generous and thoughtful person
sweetie*: NP	9	151	honey, dear, sweetheart
sweetypie*: NP	9	151	sweetheart - very affectionate
take charge of**: PV	5	75	take control
take turns: VP	7	110	share, participate fairly
talk someone's ears off: VP	5	72	talk too much about something
time-saver**: NP	8	125	convenience for busy people
tough: ADJP	8	128	hard, difficult, challenge
tube, the**NP	2	24	television, SL
turn down: PV	8	124	refuse, decrease volume
turn in: PV	9	142	give, submit, sleep